Naturally N[...] Twist Vest

Skill Level

◼◼◼◻ INTERMEDIATE

Finished Sizes

Instructions given fit 32–34-inch bust *(small)*; changes for 36–38-inch *(medium)*, 40–42-inch bust *(large)*, 44–46-inch bust *(X-large)*, 48–50-inch bust *(2X-large)*, 52–54-inch bust *(3X-large)*, and 56–58-inch bust *(4X-large)* are in [ ].

Finished Garment Measurements

Bust: 33¾ inches *(small)* [38¼ inches *(medium)*, 42¾ inches *(large)*, 47½ inches *(X-large)*, 52 inches *(2X-large)*, 56½ inches *(3X-large)*, 61¼ inches *(4X-large)*]

Length (from shoulder to bottom): 26½ inches *(small)* [26½ inches *(medium)*, 27 inches *(large)*, 27½ inches *(X-large)*, 28 inches *(2X-large)*, 28½ inches *(3X-large)*, 28½ inches *(4X-large)*]

Materials

- Red Heart Lustersheen fine (sport) weight yarn (4 oz/335 yds/113g per skein):

  2 FINE

  1 [1, 1, 1, 1, 2, 2] skein(s) #0615 tea leaf

  1 [1, 2, 2, 2, 2, 2] skein(s) #0805 natural

  1 [1, 1, 1, 1, 1, 1] skein #0332 tan
- Size F/5/3.75mm crochet hook or size needed to obtain gauge
- Tapestry needle

Gauge
[Sc, ch 5] = 1 inch; 7 rows = 2 inches

Pattern Notes
Weave in ends as work progresses.

Chain-3 at beginning of rows counts as first double crochet unless otherwise stated.

Chain-5 at beginning of rows counts as first double crochet and chain-2 space unless otherwise stated.

Chain-6 at beginning of rows counts as first double crochet and chain-3 space unless otherwise stated.

Vest is worked vertically unless otherwise stated.

Special Stitches
Cluster (cl): Insert hook in indicated st, yo, draw lp through, [insert hook in next st, yo, draw lp through] twice, yo and draw through all 4 lps on hook.

Small cluster (small cl): Insert hook in indicated st, yo, draw lp through, insert hook in next st, yo, draw lp through, yo and draw through all 3 lps on hook.

Instructions

Left Side Panel
Row 1: With tea leaf, ch 128, sc in 2nd ch from hook, *ch 5, sk next 5 chs, sc in next ch, rep from * across, **change color** (see Stitch Guide) to natural in last sc, turn. (21 ch-5 sps, 22 sc)

Row 2: Ch 1, sc in first sc, *ch 7, sk next ch-5 sp, sc in next sc, rep from * across, turn. (21 ch-7 sps, 22 sc)

Row 3: Ch 1, sc in first sc, *ch 7, sk next ch-7 sp, sc in next sc, rep from * across, change color to tea leaf in last sc, turn.

Row 4: Ch 5 (see Pattern Notes), working around next ch-7 sp, sc around ch-7 sp of 2 previous rows, *ch 5, sc around ch-7 sp of 2 previous rows, rep from * across to last ch-7 sp, sc around

ch-7 sp of 2 previous rows, turn, leaving last sc unworked. (21 ch sps, 22 sts)

Row 5: Ch 1, sc in first sc, *ch 5, sk next ch-5 sp, sc in next sc, rep from * across to beg ch-5, ch 2, sc in 3rd ch of beg ch-5, change color to tan, turn.

Row 6: Ch 6 (see Pattern Notes), sk next ch-2 sp, sc in next sc, *ch 7, sk next ch-5 sp, sc in next sc, rep from * across, turn.

Row 7: Ch 1, sc in first sc, *ch 7, sk next ch-7 sp, sc in next sc, rep from * across to beg ch-6, ch 3, sc in 3rd ch of beg ch-6, change color to tea leaf, turn.

Row 8: Ch 1, sc in first sc, *ch 5, sc around ch-7 sp of 2 previous rows, rep from * across to last ch-7 sp, sc around ch-7 sp of 2 previous rows, leaving last sc unworked. (20 ch-5 sps, 21 sc)

Row 9: Ch 1, sc in first sc, *ch 5, sk next ch-5 sp, sc in next sc, rep from * across, change color to natural, turn.

Rows 10 & 11: Rep rows 2 and 3.

Large, X-Large, 2X-Large, 3X-Large & 4X-Large Sizes Only
Row [12]: *Ch 5, sc around ch-7 sp of 2 previous rows, rep from * across to last sc, ch 2, dc in last sc, turn.

Row [13]: Ch 1, sc in first dc, ch 2, sk next ch-2 sp, *sc in next sc, ch 5, rep from * across to beg ch-5, ch 2, sc in 3rd ch of ch-5, change color to natural, turn.

Row [14]: Ch 6, sk next ch-2 sp, sc in next sc, *ch 7, sk next ch-5 sp, sc in next sc, rep from * across to last ch-2 sp, ch 3, sk last ch-2 sp, dc in last sc, turn.

Row [15]: Ch 1, sc in first dc, ch 3, sk next ch-3 sp, sc in next sc, *ch 7, sk next ch-7 sp, sc in next sc, rep from * across to beg ch-6, ch 3, sc in 3rd ch of beg ch-6, change color to tea leaf, turn.

Row [16]: Ch 1, sc in first sc, sk next ch-3 sp, *ch 5, sc around ch-7 sp

of 2 previous rows, rep from * across to last sc, sc in last sc, turn.

Row [17]: Ch 1, sc in first sc, *ch 5, sk next ch-5 sp, sc in next sc, rep from * across, change color to tan in last sc, turn.

Row [18]: Ch 1, *sc in next sc, ch 7, sk next ch-5 sp, rep from * across.

Row [19]: Ch 1, sc in first sc, *ch 7, sk next ch-7, sc in next sc, rep from * across, turn.

2X-Large, 3X-Large & 4X-Large Sizes Only
Rows [20–28, 20–36, 20–44]: [Rep rows 12–19 consecutively] [1, 2, 3] time(s).

All Sizes
Row 12 [12, 20, 20, 29, 37, 45]: *Ch 5, sc around ch-7 sp of 2 previous rows, rep from * across to last sc, ch 2, dc in last sc, turn.

Row 13 [13, 21, 21, 30, 38, 46]: Ch 1, sc in first dc, ch 2, sk next ch-2 sp, *sc in next sc, ch 5, sk next ch-5 sp, rep from * across to beg ch-5, ch 2, sc in 3rd ch of beg ch-5, change color to tan, turn.

Row 14 [14, 22, 22, 31, 39, 47]: Ch 6, sk next ch-2 sp, *sc in next sc, ch 7, sk next ch-5 sp, rep from * across to last sc, sc in last sc, ch 7, sk next ch-2 sp, dc in last sc, turn.

Row 15 [15, 23, 23, 32, 40, 48]: Ch 1, sc in first dc, *ch 7, sk next ch-7 sp, sc in next sc, rep from * across to beg ch-6, ch 3, sc in 3rd ch of beg ch-6, change color to tea leaf, turn.

Row 16 [16, 24, 24, 33, 41, 49]: Ch 1, sc in first sc, sk next ch-3 sp, *ch 5, sc around ch-7 sp of 2 previous rows, rep from * across, ch 2, dc in last sc, turn.

Row 17 [17, 25, 25, 34, 42, 50]: Ch 1, sc in first dc, ch 2, sk next ch-2 sp, *sc in next sc, ch 5, sk next ch-5 sp, rep from * across, change color to natural in last sc, turn.

Row 18 [18, 26, 26, 35, 43, 51]: Ch 1, sc in first sc, *ch 7, sk next

ch-5 sp, sc in next sc, rep from * across, ending ch 7, sk ch-2 sp, dc in last sc, turn.

Row 19 [19, 27, 27, 36, 44, 52]: Ch 1, sc in first dc, *ch 7, sk next ch-7 sp, sc in next sc, rep from * across, change to tea leaf in last sc, turn.

Left Shoulder

Row 1: *Ch 5, sc around ch-7 sp of 2 previous rows, rep from * across to last sc, ch 5, sc in last sc, ch 59 [59, 65, 71, 77, 83, 83], sl st in first sc of row 1 *(armhole made)*, turn.

Row 2: *Ch 5, sk next 5 ch, sc in next ch, rep from * across, **sc in next sc, ch 5, sk next ch-5 sp, rep from ** across to beg ch-5, ch 2, sc in 3rd ch of beg ch-5, change color to tan, turn. *(30 [30, 31, 32, 33, 34, 34] ch sps)*

Row 3: Ch 6, sk next ch-2 sp, *sc in next sc, ch 7, sk next ch-5 sp, rep from * across to sl st of row 1, sc in sl st, working in unused lps on opposite side of foundation ch, *ch 7, sk next 5 chs, sc in next ch, rep from ** across, turn. *(53 [53, 54, 55, 56, 57, 57] ch sps, 53 53, 54, 55, 56, 57, 57] sts)*

Row 4: Ch 1, sc in first sc, *ch 7, sk next ch-7 sp, sc in next sc, rep from * across to beg ch-6, ch 3, sc in 3rd ch of beg ch-6, change color to tea leaf, turn.

Row 5: Ch 1, sc in first sc, sk next ch-3 sp, *ch 5, sc around ch-7 sp of 2 previous rows, rep from * across to last sc, ch 2, dc in last sc, turn.

Row 6: Ch 1, sc in first dc, ch 2, sk next ch-2 sp, *sc in next sc, ch 5, sk next ch-5 sp, rep from * across, change color to natural in last sc, turn.

Row 7: Ch 1, sc in first sc, *ch 7, sk next ch-5 sp, sc in next sc, rep from * across, ch 3, sk ch-2 sp, dc in last sc, turn.

Row 8: Ch 1, sc in dc, ch 3, sk next ch-3 sp, *sc in next sc, ch 7, sk next ch-7 sp, rep from * across,

change color to tea leaf in last sc, turn.

Row 9: *Ch 5, sc around ch-7 sp of 2 previous rows, rep from * across to last sc, sc in last sc, turn.

Row 10: Ch 1, sc in first sc, *ch 5, sk next ch-5 sp, sc in next sc, rep from * across to beg ch-5, ch 2, sc in 3rd ch of beg ch-5, change to tan, turn.

Row 11: Ch 6, sk next ch-2 sp, *sc in next sc, ch 7, sk next ch-5 sp, rep from * across, turn.

Rows 12–14: Rep rows 4–6.

Small, Medium & Large Sizes Only

At end of last row, do not change color. Fasten off.

X-Large, 2X-Large, 3X-Large & 4X-Large Sizes Only

Rows [15–18]: Rep rows 7–10. At end of last row, do not change color. Fasten off.

Back
Small, Medium & Large Sizes Only

Row 1 (WS): Hold piece with WS facing, sk first 28 sc of Left Shoulder, join natural with sl st in next sc, sc in same sc, *ch 7, sk next ch-5 sp, sc in next sc, rep from * across to last ch-2 sp, ch 3, sk last ch-2 sp, dc in last sc, turn. *(25 [25, 26] ch sps, 26 [26, 26] sts)*

Row 2: Ch 1, sc in first dc, ch 3, sk next ch-3 sp, *sc in next sc, ch 7, sk next ch-7 sp, rep from * across, change to tea leaf in last sc, turn.

Row 3: *Ch 5, sc around ch-7 sp of 2 previous rows, rep from * across to last ch-3 sp, ch 5, sk last ch-3 sp, sc in last sc, turn.

Row 4: Ch 1, sc in first sc, *ch 5, sk next ch-5 sp, sc in next sc, rep from * across to last sc, sc in last sc, sc in 3rd ch of beg ch-5, change to tan, turn.

Row 5: Ch 1, sk first sc, *sc in next sc, ch 7, sk next ch-5 sp, rep from * across. *(24 [24, 25] ch sps, 25 [25, 26] sc)*

Row 6: Ch 1, sc in first sc, *ch 7, sk next ch-7, sc in next sc, rep from * across, change to tea leaf in last sc, turn.

Row 7: *Ch 5, sc around ch-7 sp of 2 previous rows, rep from * across to last sc, ch 2, dc in last sc, turn.

Row 8: Ch 1, sc in first dc, ch 2, sk ch-2 sp, *sc in next sc, ch 5, rep from * across to beg ch-5, ch 2, sc in 3rd ch of beg ch-5, change to natural, turn.

Row 9: Ch 6, sk next ch-2 sp, sc in next sc, *ch 7, sk next ch-5 sp, sc in next sc, rep from * across to last ch-2 sp, ch 3, sk last ch-2 sp, dc in last sc, turn.

Row 10: Ch 1, sc in first dc, ch 3, sk next ch-3 sp, sc in next sc, *ch 7, sk next ch-7 sp, sc in next sc, rep from * across to beg ch-6, ch 3, sc in 3rd ch of beg ch-6, change color to tea leaf, turn.

Row 11: Ch 1, sc in first sc, sk next ch-3 sp, *ch 5, sc around ch-7 sp of 2 previous rows, rep from * across to last sc, sc in last sc, turn.

Row 12: Ch 1, sc in first sc, *ch 5, sk next ch-5 sp, sc in next sc, rep from * across, change color to tan, turn.

Small Size Only

Rows 13–15: Rep rows 5–7.

Row 16: Ch 1, sc in first dc, ch 2, sk next ch-2 sp, *sc in next sc, ch 5, rep from * across to beg ch-5, ch 5, sc in 3rd ch of beg ch-5, change color to natural, turn.

Row 17: Ch 1, sc in first sc, *ch 7, sk next ch-5 sp, sc in next sc, rep from * across to last ch-2 sp, ch 3, sk last ch-2 sp, dc in last sc, turn.

Row 18: Ch 1, sc in first dc, ch 3, sk next ch-3 sp, *sc in next sc, ch 7, sk next ch-7 sp, rep from * across to last sc, sc in last sc, change to tea leaf, turn.

Row 19: Ch 8, sc in first 2 ch-7 sps of previous 2 rows, *ch 5, sc around ch-7 sp of 2 previous rows, rep from * across, sc in last sc.

Row 20: Ch 1, sc in first sc, *ch 5, sk next ch-5 sp, sc in next sc, rep from * across to beg ch-8, ch 5, sc in 3rd ch of beg ch-8, ch 166, sc in 2nd ch from hook, ch 2, sk next 2 chs, **sc in next sc, ch 5, sk next 5 chs, rep from ** across ch, sl st in next sc, fasten off. *(24 ch sps)*

Medium & Large Sizes Only
Rows [13–20]: Rep rows 5–12.
Rows [21–23]: Rep rows 5–7.
Row [24]: Ch 1, sc in first dc, ch 2, sk next ch-2 sp, *sc in next sc, ch 5, rep from * across to beg ch-5, ch 5, sc in 3rd ch of ch-5, change color to natural, turn.
Row [25]: Ch 1, sc in first sc, *ch 7, sk next ch-5 sp, sc in next sc, rep from * across to last ch-2 sp, ch 3, sk last ch-2 sp, dc in last sc, turn.
Row [26]: Ch 1, sc in first dc, ch 3, sk next ch-3 sp, *sc in next sc, ch 7, sk next ch-7 sp, rep from * across, ending sc in last sc, change to tea leaf, turn.
Row [27]: Ch 8, sc in first 2 ch-7 sps of previous 2 rows, *ch 5, sc around ch-7 sp of 2 previous rows, rep from * across, ending sc in last sc.
Row [28]: Ch 1, sc in first sc, *ch 5, sk next ch-5 sp, sc in next sc, rep from * across, ch 5, sc in 3rd ch of ch-8, ch [166, 172], sc in 2nd ch from hook, ch 2, sk next 2 chs, **sc in next sc, ch 5, sk next 5 chs, rep from ** across, sl st in next sc, fasten off. *(25 ch sps)*

X-Large, 2X-Large, 3X-Large & 4X-Large Sizes Only
Row [1] (WS): Hold piece with WS facing, sk first 28 sc, join tan with sl st in next sc, ch 6, sk next ch-2 sp, *sc in next sc, ch 7, sk next ch-5 sp, rep from * across, turn. *([27, 28, 29, 29] ch sps, [28, 29, 30, 30] sc)*
Row [2]: Ch 1, sc in first sc, *ch 7, sk next ch-7 sp, sc in next sc, rep from * across, ch 3, sc in 3rd ch

of beg ch-6, change color to tea leaf, turn.
Row [3]: Ch 1, sc in first sc, sk next ch-3 sp, *ch 5, sc around ch-7 sp of 2 previous rows, rep from * across to last sc, ch 2, dc in last sc, turn. *([26, 27, 28, 28] ch sps, [27, 28, 29, 29] sc)*
Row [4]: Ch 1, sc in first dc, ch 2, sk ch-2 sp, *sc in next sc, ch 5, sk next ch-5 sp, rep from * across, change color to natural in last sc, turn.
Row [5]: Ch 1, sc in first sc, *ch 7, sk next ch-5 sp, sc in next sc, rep from * across to last ch-2 sp, ch 3, sk last ch-2 sp, dc in last sc, turn.
Row [6]: Ch 1, sc in first dc, ch 3, sk next ch-3 sp, *sc in next sc, ch 7, sk next ch-7 sp, rep from * across, change color to tea leaf in last sc, turn.
Row [7]: *Ch 5, sc around ch-7 sp of 2 previous rows, rep from * across to last sc, sc in last sc, turn.
Row [8]: Ch 1, sc in first sc, *ch 5, sk next ch-5 sp, sc in next sc, rep from * across to beg ch-5, ch 2, sc in 3rd ch of beg ch-5, change color to tan, turn.
Row [9]: Ch 6, sk next ch-2 sp, *sc in next sc, ch 7, sk next ch-5 sp, rep from * across, turn.
Rows [10–17]: Rep rows 2–9.
Rows [18–23]: Rep rows 2–7.
Row [24]: Ch 1, sc in first sc, *ch 5, sk next ch-5 sp, sc in next sc, rep from * across to beg ch-5, ch 5, sc in 3rd ch of beg ch-5, change color to tan, turn.
Row [25]: Ch 6, sc in first sc, *ch 7, sk next ch-5 sp, sc in next sc, rep from * across, turn.
Row [26]: Ch 1, sc in first sc, *ch 7, sk next ch-7 sp, sc in next sc, rep from * across to beg ch-6, ch 3, sc in 3rd ch of beg ch-6, change color to tea leaf, turn.
Row [27]: Ch 1, sc in first sc, sk next ch-3 sp, *ch 5, sc around ch-7 sp of 2 previous rows, rep from * across to last sc, ch 2, dc in last sc, turn. *([27, 28, 28] ch sps, [28, 29, 29] sc)*

Row [28]: Ch 1, sc in first dc, ch 2, sk ch-2 sp, *sc in next sc, ch 5, sk next ch-5 sp, rep from * across to last sc, ch 5, sc in last sc, ch [178, 184, 190, 190], sc in 2nd ch from hook, ch 2, sk next 2 chs, **sc in next sc, ch 5, sk next 5 chs, rep from ** across ch, sl st in next sc, fasten off.

Right Shoulder
Small, Medium & Large Sizes Only
Row 1: Join tan with sl st in first sc of lower edge, ch 6, sk next ch-2 sp, *sc in next sc, ch 7, sk next ch-5 sp, rep from * across, turn.
Row 2: Ch 1, sc in first sc, *ch 7, sk next ch-7 sp, sc in next sc, rep from * across to beg ch-6, ch 3, sc in 3rd ch of beg ch-6, change color to tea leaf, turn.
Row 3: Ch 1, sc in first sc, *ch 5, sc around ch-7 sp of 2 previous rows, rep from * across, to last sc, ch 2, dc in last sc, turn.
Row 4: Ch 1, sc in first dc, ch 2, sk next ch-2 sp, *sc in next sc, ch 5, sk next ch-5 sp, rep from * across, change color to natural, turn.
Rows 5–12: Rep rows 7–14 of Left Shoulder.

X-Large, 2X-Large, 3X-Large & 4X-Large Sizes Only
Row 1: Join natural with sl st in first sc at lower edge, ch 1, sc in same sc, *ch 7, sk next ch-5 sp, sc in next sc, rep from * across to last ch-2 sp, ch 3, sk last ch-2 sp, dc in last sc, turn.
Row 2: Ch 1, sc in first dc, ch 3, sk next ch-3 sp, *sc in next sc, ch 7, sk next ch-7 sp, rep from * across, change color to tea leaf in last sc, turn.
Row 3: *Ch 5, sc around ch-7 sp of 2 previous rows, rep from * across, ending sc in last sc, turn.
Row 4: Ch 1, sc in first sc, *ch 5, sk next ch-5 sp, sc in next sc, rep from * across to beg ch-5, ch 2, sc in 3rd ch of ch-5, change color to tan, turn.

Row 5: Ch 6, sk next ch-2 sp, *sc in next sc, ch 7, sk next ch-5 sp, rep from * across, turn.

Row 6: Ch 1, sc in first sc, *ch 7, sk next ch-7 sp, sc in next sc, rep from * across to beg ch-6, ch 3, sc in 3rd ch of ch-6, change color to tea leaf, turn.

Row 7: Ch 1, sc in first sc, *ch 5, sc around ch-7 sp of 2 previous rows, rep from * across to last sc, ch 2, dc in last sc, turn.

Row 8: Ch 1, sc in first dc, ch 2, sk ch-2 sp, *sc in next sc, ch 5, sk next ch-5 sp, rep from * across, turn.

Rows 9–16: Rep rows 7–14 of Left Shoulder.

Right Side Panel
All Sizes
Row 1: Ch 1, sc in first sc, *ch 7, sk next ch-5 sp, sc in next sc, rep from * across, turn. *(21 ch-7 sps, 22 sc)*

Row 2: Ch 1, sc in first sc, *ch 7, sk next ch-7 sp, sc in next sc, rep from * across, change color to tea leaf in last sc, turn.

Row 3: Ch 5, sc around ch-7 sp of 2 previous rows, *ch 5, sc around ch-7 sp of 2 previous rows, rep from * across to last ch-7 sp, sc around ch-7 sp of 2 previous rows, turn, leaving last sc unworked. *(21 ch sps, 22 sts)*

Row 4: Ch 1, sc in first sc, *ch 5, sk next ch-5 sp, sc in next sc, rep from * across to beg ch-5, ch 2, sc in 3rd ch of beg ch-5, change color to tan, turn.

Row 5: Ch 6, sk next ch-2 sp, sc in next sc, *ch 7, sk next ch-5 sp, sc in next sc, rep from * across, turn.

Row 6: Ch 1, sc in first sc, *ch 7, sk next ch-7 sp, sc in next sc, rep from * across to beg ch-6, ch 3, sc in 3rd ch of beg ch-6, change color to tea leaf, turn.

Row 7: Ch 1, sc in first sc, *ch 5, sc around ch-7 sp of 2 previous rows, rep from * across to last ch-7 sp, sc around ch-7 sp of 2 previous rows, turn, leaving last sc unworked. *(20 ch-5 sps, 21 sc)*

Row 8: Ch 1, sc in first sc, *ch 5, sk next ch-5 sp, sc in next sc, rep from * across, change color to natural, turn.

Rows 9 & 10: Rep rows 1 and 2. *(20 ch sps, 21 sc at end of row 9)*

Large, X-Large, 2X-Large, 3X-Large & 4X-Large Sizes Only
Row [11]: *Ch 5, sc around ch-7 sp of 2 previous rows, rep from * across to last sc, ch 2, dc in last sc, turn.

Row [12]: Ch 1, sc in first dc, ch 2, sk next ch-2 sp, *sc in next sc, ch 5, rep from * across to beg ch-5, ch 2, sc in 3rd ch of beg ch-5, change color to natural, turn.

Row [13]: Ch 6, sk next ch-2 sp, sc in next sc, *ch 7, sk next ch-5 sp, sc in next sc, rep from * across to last ch-2 sp, ch 3, sk last ch-2 sp, dc in last sc, turn.

Row [14]: Ch 1, sc in first dc, ch 3, sk next ch-3 sp, sc in next sc, *ch 7, sk next ch-7 sp, sc in next sc, rep from * across to beg ch-6, ch 3, sc in 3rd ch of beg ch-6, change color to tea leaf, turn.

Row [15]: Ch 1, sc in first sc, sk next ch-3 sp, *ch 5, sc around ch-7 sp of 2 previous rows, rep from * across to last sc, sc in last sc, turn.

Row [16]: Ch 1, sc in first sc, *ch 5, sk next ch-5 sp, sc in next sc, rep from * across, change color to tan in last sc, turn.

Row [17]: Ch 1, *sc in next sc, ch 7, sk next ch-5 sp, rep from * across.

Row [18]: Ch 1, sc in first sc, *ch 7, sk next ch-7, sc in next sc, rep from * across, turn.

2X-Large, 3X-Large & 4X-Large Sizes Only
Rows [19–27, 20–35, 19–43]: [Rep rows 11–18 consecutively] [1, 2, 3] times.

All Sizes
Row 11 [11, 19, 19, 28, 36, 44]: *Ch 5, sc around ch-7 sp of 2 previous rows, rep from * across to last sc, ch 2, dc in last sc, turn.

Row 12 [12, 20, 20, 29, 37, 45]: Ch 1, sc in first dc, ch 2, sk next ch-2 sp, *sc in next sc, ch 5, sk next ch-5 sp, rep from * across to beg ch-5, ch 2, sc in 3rd ch of beg ch-5, change color to tan, turn.

Row 13 [13, 21, 21, 32, 38, 46]: Ch 6, sk next ch-2 sp, *sc in next sc, ch 7, sk next ch-5 sp, rep from * across to last sc, sc in last sc, ch 7, sk next ch-2 sp, dc in last sc, turn.

Row 14 [14, 22, 22, 33, 39, 47]: Ch 1, sc in first dc, *ch 7, sk next ch-7 sp, sc in next sc, rep from * across to beg ch-6, ch 3, sc in 3rd ch of beg ch-6, change color to tea leaf, turn.

Row 15 [15, 23, 23, 32, 40, 48]: Ch 1, sc in first sc, sk next ch-3 sp, *ch 5, sc around ch-7 sp of 2 previous rows, rep from * across, ending ch 2, dc in last sc, turn.

Row 16 [16, 24, 24, 33, 41, 49]: Ch 1, sc in first dc, ch 2, sk next ch-2 sp, *sc in next sc, ch 5, sk next ch-5 sp, rep from * across, change color to natural in last sc, turn.

Row 17 [17, 25, 25, 34, 42, 50]: Working on WS of Panel and RS of Right Shoulder/Back, ch 1, sc in first sc of Panel, ch 2, sc in corresponding sc of Right Shoulder/Back, ch 2, sl st in first sc of Panel, *ch 3, sc in next sc of Right Shoulder/Back**, ch 3, sc in next sc of Panel, rep from * across, ending last rep at **, turn.

Row 18 [18, 26, 26, 35, 43, 51]: *Ch 3, sk next ch-3 sp, sl st in next sc, rep from * across to last sc of Right Shoulder/Back, ch 2, sl st in last sc of Right Shoulder/Back, fasten off.

Left Side Extension
Row 1: Hold piece with WS facing and Left Side Panel edge at top, join natural with sl st in first sc in right-hand corner, ch 1, sc in same sc, [ch 7, sk next ch-5 sp, sc in next sc] 22 [22, 23, 24, 25, 26, 26] times, turn. *(22 [22, 23, 24, 25, 26, 26] ch sps, 23 [23, 24, 25, 26, 27, 27] sc)*

Row 2: Ch 1, sc in first sc, *ch 7, sk next ch-7 sp, sc in next sc, rep from * across, change color to tea leaf in last sc, turn.

Row 3: *Ch 5, sc around ch-7 sp of 2 previous rows, rep from * across to last ch-7 sp, sc in last ch-7 sp on 2nd row below, turn.

Small Size Only

Row 4: Ch 1, sc in first sc, *ch 5, sk next ch-5 sp, sc in next sc, rep from * across to beg ch-5, ch 2, sc in 3rd ch of beg ch-5, fasten off.

Medium, Large, X-Large, 2X-Large, 3X-Large & 4X-Large Sizes Only

Row [4]: Ch 1, sc in first sc, *ch 5, sk next ch-5 sp, sc in next sc, rep from * across to beg ch-5, ch 2, sc in 3rd ch of beg ch-5, change color to tan, turn.

Row [5]: Ch 6, sk next ch-2 sp, sc in next sc, [ch 7, sk next ch-5 sp, sc in next sc] [20, 21, 22, 23, 24, 24] times, turn. *([21, 22, 23, 24, 25, 25] ch sps, [22, 23, 24, 25, 26, 26] sc)*

Row [6]: Ch 1, sc in first sc, *ch 7, sk next ch-7 sp, sc in next sc, rep from * across to beg ch-6, ch 3, sc in 3rd ch of ch-6, change color to tea leaf, turn.

Row [7]: Ch 1, sc in first sc, sk next ch-3 sp, *ch 5, sc around ch-7 sp of 2 previous rows, rep from * across to last sc, ch 5, sc in last sc, ch 5, working across next side in ends of rows, sc in sc at end of row 4, ch 5, sc in sc at end of row 2, sk next row, tr in sc at end of next row of Left Side Panel, turn. *([24, 25, 26, 27, 28, 28] sps)*

Row [8]: Ch 1, sc in first sc, *ch 5, sk next ch-5 sp, sc in next sc, rep from * across, fasten off. *([23, 24,*

25, 26, 27, 27] ch sps, [24, 25, 26, 27, 28, 28] sc)

Right Side Extension

Row 1: Hold piece with RS facing and Right Side Panel edge at top, working in unused lps on opposite side of ch made on last row of Back, join natural with sl st in first ch, ch 6, sk next ch-2 sp, [sc in next ch, ch 7, sk next ch-5 sp] 22 times, turn. *(23 [24, 25, 25, 26, 27, 27] ch sps, 24 [25, 26, 26, 27, 28, 28] sts)*

Row 2: Ch 1, sc in first sc, *ch 7, sk next ch-7 sp, sc in next sc, rep from * across to beg ch-6, ch 3, sc in 3rd ch of ch-6, change color to tea leaf, turn.

Row 3: Ch 1, sc in first sc, sk next ch-3 sp, *ch 5, sc around ch-7 sp of 2 previous rows, rep from * across to last ch-7 sp, sc around ch-7 sp of 2 previous rows, turn.

Small Size Only

Row 4: Ch 1, sc in first sc, *ch 5, sk next ch-5 sp, sc in next sc, rep from * across, fasten off.

Medium, Large, X-Large, 2X-Large, 3X-Large & 4X-Large Sizes Only

Row 4: Ch 1, sc in first sc, *ch 5, sk next ch-5 sp, sc in next sc, rep from * across, change to tan, turn.

Row 5: Ch 1, sc in same st, * ch 7, sk next ch-5 sp, sc in next sc, rep from * [19, 20, 21, 22, 23, 23] times, turn. *([20, 21, 22, 23, 24, 24] ch sps, [21, 22, 23, 24, 25, 25] sc)*

Row 6: Ch 1, sc in first sc, *ch 7, sk next ch-7 sp, sc in next sc, rep from * across, change to tea leaf in last sc, turn.

Row 7: *Ch 5, sc around ch-7 sp

of 2 previous rows, rep from * across to last sc, ch 5, sc in last sc, ch 5, working across next side in ends of rows, sc in sc at end of row 4, ch 5, sc in sc at end of row 2, sk next row, tr in sc at end of next row, turn. *([24, 25, 26, 27, 28, 28] sps)*

Row 8: Ch 1, sc in first sc, *ch 5, sk next ch-5 sp, sc in next sc, rep from * across to beg ch-5, ch 2, sc in 3rd ch of ch-5, turn.

Edgings
Outer Edging

Working along Right Side Panel edge, 3 sc in first sc, 2 sc in next ch-2 sp, *5 sc in each ch-5 sp**, rep from * to next tr, 4 sc in next tr, 5 sc in each ch-5 sp across to Back neck edge, sc evenly spaced across to ch-5 sp at top of Left Front Panel edge, 5 sc in ch-5 sp and in each rem ch-5 sp across Left Front Panel edge to last sc, 3 sc in last sc, working across lower edge, sc evenly spaced across to beg sc, sl st in beg sc, fasten off.

Armhole Edging

Hold 1 Armhole with RS facing, join tea leaf in center of underarm, ch 1, sc evenly spaced to next ch-5 sp, working around armhole, 5 sc in each ch-5 sp, sc evenly spaced to beg sc, sl st in beg sc. Rep around other armhole.

Ties

With 2 strands held tog, join tea leaf with sl st in 3rd sc of 21st [21st, 22nd, 23rd, 24th, 25th, 25th] ch sp from lower edge of Right Side Extension, ch 45, fasten off. Rep for Tie on Left Side Extension. ■

Cut Diamond Cardigan

Skill Level

■■■□ INTERMEDIATE

Finished Sizes

Instructions given fit 32–34-inch bust *(small)*; changes for 36–38-inch *(medium)*, 40–42-inch bust *(large)*, 44–46-inch bust *(X-large)*, 48–50-inch bust *(2X-large)*, 52–54-inch bust *(3X-large)*, and 56–58-inch bust *(4X-large)* are in [ ].

Finished Garment Measurements

Bust: 40 inches *(small)* [44 inches *(medium)*, 48 inches *(large)*, 52 inches *(X-large)*, 56 inches *(2X-large)*, 60 inches *(3X-large)*, 64 inches *(4X-large)*]

Length (from shoulder to bottom): 28 inches *(small)* [30 inches *(medium)*, 31 inches *(large)*, 33 inches *(X-large)*, 34 inches *(2X-large)*, 36 inches *(3X-large)*, 36 inches *(4X-large)*]

Materials

- TLC Cotton Plus medium (worsted) weight yarn (3 oz/153 yds/85g per skein): 7 [8, 9, 9, 10, 11, 12] skeins #3324 thistle multi
- Size H/8/5mm crochet hook or size needed to obtain gauge
- Tapestry needle

Gauge

2 rows = 1 inch
1 rep of (picot, ch 3, dc, ch 3, picot) or (picot, shell) = 2 inches

Pattern Notes

Weave in ends as work progresses.

Chain-3 at beginning of double crochet rows counts as first double crochet unless otherwise stated.

Chain-6 at beginning of double crochet row counts as first double crochet and chain-3 space unless otherwise stated.

Special Stitches

Beginning picot (beg picot): (Ch 3, sc) in indicated st.

Picot: (Sc, ch 3, sc) in indicated st.

Ending picot: (Sc, ch 1, hdc) in indicated st.

Shell: 5 dc in indicated sp.

Instructions

Right Sleeve

Row 1 (WS): Beg at lower edge of sleeve, ch 49 [49, 56, 56, 63, 63, 63], sc in 10th ch from hook *(beg 9 sk chs count as a dc and a ch-3 sp)*, *ch 3, sc in next ch, ch 3, sk next 2 ch, dc in next ch**, ch 3, sk next 2 ch, sc in next ch, rep from * across, ending last rep at **, turn. *(18 [18, 21, 21, 24, 24, 24] ch-3 sps, 12 [12, 14, 14, 16, 16, 16] sc, 7 [7, 8, 8, 9, 9, 9] dc)*

Row 2 (RS): Beg picot *(see Special Stitches)* in first dc, *ch 3, sk next ch-3 sp, dc in next ch-3 sp, ch 3, **picot** *(see Special Stitches)* in next dc, rep from * across to beg 9 sk chs, sk next 3 ch, **ending picot** *(see Special Stitches)* in next ch, turn, leaving rem chs unworked. *(7 [7, 8, 8, 9, 9, 9] picots, 12 [12, 14, 14, 16, 16, 16] ch-3 sps, 6 [6, 7, 7, 8, 8, 8] dc)*

Row 3: Ch 6 *(see Pattern Notes)*, *picot in next dc, ch 3, dc in ch-3 sp of next picot, ch 3, rep from * across to last picot, dc in ch-3 sp of last picot, turn. *(6 [6, 7, 7, 8, 8, 8] picots, 12 [12, 14, 14, 16, 16, 16] ch-3 sps, 7 [7, 8, 8, 9, 9, 9] dc)*

Row 4: Ch 6, sc in first dc, *ch 3, dc in ch-3 sp of next picot, ch 3, picot in next dc, rep from * across to last dc, ch 3, (sc, ch 3, dc) in last dc, turn. *(5 [5, 6, 6, 7, 7, 7] picots, 14 [14, 16, 16, 18, 18, 18] ch-3 sps, 8 [8, 9, 9, 10, 10, 10] dc, 2 sc)*

Row 5: Beg picot in first dc, ch 3, dc in 2nd ch of next ch-3 sp, *ch 3, picot in next dc, ch 3, dc in ch-3 sp of next picot, rep from * across to last sc, ch 3, sk last sc, sk next ch, dc in next ch, ch 3, sk next ch, ending picot in next ch, turn. *(8 [8, 9, 9, 10, 10, 10] picots, 14 [14, 16, 16, 18, 18, 18] ch-3 sps, 7 [7, 8, 8, 9, 9, 9] dc)*

Row 6: Ch 6, *picot in next dc, ch 3, dc in ch-3 sp of next picot, ch 3, rep from * across to last picot, ch 3, dc in ch-3 sp of last picot, turn. *(7 [7, 8, 8, 9, 9, 9] picots, 14 [14, 16, 16, 18, 18, 18] ch-3 sps, 8 [8, 9, 9, 10, 10, 10] dc)*

Row 7: Beg picot in first dc, *ch 3, dc in ch-3 sp of next picot, ch 3, picot in next dc, rep from * across to beg ch-6, ending picot in 3rd ch of beg ch-6, turn. *(8 [8,*

   American School of Needlework • Berne, Indiana 46711 • DRGnetwork.com

9, 9, 10, 10, 10] picots, 14 [14, 16, 16, 18, 18, 18] ch-3 sps, 7 [7, 8, 8, 9, 9, 9] dc)

Rows 8 & 9 [8 & 9, 8–11, 8–11, 8 & 9, 8 & 9, 8 & 9]: [Rep rows 6 and 7 alternately] 1 [1, 2, 2, 1, 1, 1] time(s).

Rows 10–12 [10–12, 12–14, 12–14, 10–12, 10–12, 10–12]: Rep rows 3–5. (9 [9, 10, 10, 11, 11, 11] picots, 16 [16, 18, 18, 20, 20, 20] ch-3 sps at end of last row)

Rows 13–16 [13–16, 15–18, 15–18, 13–16, 13–16, 13–16]: [Rep rows 6 and 7 alternately] twice.

Rows 17–19 [17–19, 19–21, 19–21, 17–19, 17–19, 17–19]: Rep rows 3–5. (10 [10, 11, 11, 12, 12, 12] picots, 18 [18, 20, 20, 22, 22, 22] ch-3 sps at end of last row)

Rows 20–25 [20–27, 22–29, 22–31, 20–29, 20–31, 20–31]: [Rep rows 6 and 7 alternately] 3 [4, 4, 5, 5, 6, 6] times. At end of last row, fasten off.

Right Body

Row 1 (WS) Ch 66 [73, 73, 80, 80, 87, 87], with WS facing, dc in first hdc of last row of Sleeve, *ch 3, picot in next dc, ch 3, dc in ch-3 sp of next picot, rep from * across, dc in last picot, ch 72 [79, 79, 86, 86, 93, 93], turn.

Row 2 (RS): Sc in 10th ch from hook, ch 3, sc in next ch, ◊*ch 3, sk next 2 chs, dc in next ch, [ch 3, sk next 2 chs, sc in next ch] twice◊, rep from * across to last 3 chs, dc in next ch, sk last 2 chs, ** ch 3, picot in next dc, ch 3, dc in next picot, rep from ** across sleeve, picot in last dc, rep between ◊◊ across to last ch, dc in last ch, turn. (28 [30, 31, 33, 34, 36, 36] picots, 56 [60, 62, 66, 68, 72, 72] ch-3 sps)

Row 3: Beg picot in first dc, [**shell** (see Special Stitches) in ch-3 sp of next picot, picot in next dc] 10 [11, 11, 12, 12, 13, 13] times, [ch 3, dc in ch-3 sp of next picot, ch 3, picot in next dc] 8 [8, 9, 9, 10,

10, 10] times, *shell in ch-3 sp of next picot, picot in next dc, rep from * across to last 4 chs, sk next 3 chs, ending picot in last ch, turn. (20 [22, 22, 24, 24, 26, 26] shells, 29 [31, 32, 34, 35, 37, 37] picots, 16 [16, 18, 18, 20, 20, 20] ch-3 sps)

Row 4: Ch 6, [picot in 3rd dc of next shell, ch 3, dc in ch-3 sp of next picot, ch 3] 10 [11, 11, 12, 12, 13, 13] times, [picot in next dc, ch 3, dc in ch-3 sp of next picot, ch 3] 8 [8, 9, 9, 10, 10, 10] times, *picot in 3rd dc of next shell, ch 3, dc in ch-3 sp of next picot, ch 3, rep from * across to last picot, dc in last picot, turn.

Row 5: Beg picot in first dc, [shell in ch-3 sp of next picot, picot in next dc] 10 [11, 11, 12, 12, 13, 13] times, [ch 3, dc in ch-3 sp of next picot, ch 3, picot in next dc] 8 [8, 9, 9, 10, 10, 10] times, *shell in ch-3 sp of next picot, picot in next dc, rep from * across to last dc, ending picot in last dc, turn.

Rows 6–13 [6–15, 6–17, 6–17, 6–19, 6–19, 6–21]: [Rep rows 4 and 5 alternately] 4 [5, 6, 6, 7, 7, 8] times.

Back

Row 1: Ch 6, [picot in 3rd dc of next shell, ch 3, dc in ch-3 sp of next picot, ch 3] 10 [11, 11, 12, 12, 13, 13] times, [picot in next dc, ch 3, dc in ch-3 sp of next picot, ch 3] 2 [2, 2, 2, 3, 3, 3] times, *picot in next dc, ch 3, dc in ch-3 sp of next picot, leaving rem sts unworked, turn. (13 [14, 14, 15, 16, 17, 17] picots, 26 [28, 28, 30, 32, 34, 34] ch-3 sps)

Row 2: Beg picot in first dc, [ch 3, dc in ch-3 sp of next picot, ch 3, picot in next dc] 3 [3, 4, 4, 5, 5, 5] times, *shell in ch-3 sp of next picot, picot in next dc, rep from * across to last dc, ending picot in last dc, turn. (10 [11, 11, 12, 12, 13, 13] shells, 14 [15, 15, 16, 17, 18, 18] picots, 6 [6, 6, 6, 8, 8, 8] ch-3 sps)

Row 3: Ch 6, [picot in 3rd dc of

next shell, ch 3, dc inch-3 sp of next picot, ch 3] 10 [11, 11, 12, 12, 13, 13] times, *picot in next dc, ch 3, dc in ch-3 sp of next picot, ch 3, rep from * across to last picot, dc in ch-3 sp of last picot, turn.

Rows 4–13 [4–15, 4–17, 4–19, 4–19, 4–23, 4–25]: [Rep rows 2 and 3 alternately] 5 [6, 7, 8, 8, 10, 11] times. At end of last row, fasten off.

Right Front

Row 1: Hold piece with WS facing, sk 10 [10, 12, 12, 12, 12, 12] ch-3 sps from Back, join yarn with sl st in ch-3 sp of next picot, ch 6, *picot in 3rd dc of next shell, ch 3, dc in ch-3 sp of next picot, ch 3, rep from * across to last picot, dc in ch-3 sp of last picot, turn. (10 [11, 11, 12, 12, 13, 13] picots, 20 [22, 22, 24, 24, 26, 26] ch-3 sps)

Row 2: Beg picot in first dc, *shell in ch-3 sp of next picot, picot in next dc, rep from * across to last dc, ending picot in last dc, turn. (10 [11, 11, 12, 12, 13, 13] shells, 11 [12, 12, 13, 13, 14, 14] picots)

Row 3: Ch 4, sc in ch-3 sp of next shell, *ch 3, dc in ch-3 sp of next picot, ch 3, picot in 3rd dc of next shell, rep from * across to last picot, dc in ch-3 sp of last picot, turn.

Row 4: Beg picot in first dc, *shell in ch-3 sp of next picot, picot in next dc, rep from * across to last dc, ending picot in last dc, turn. (9 [10, 10, 11, 11, 12, 12] shells, 10 [11, 11, 12, 12, 13, 13] picots)

Rows 5 & 6 [5–8, 5–8, 5–10, 5–10, 5–12, 5–12]: [Rep rows 3 and 4 alternately] 1 [2, 2, 3, 3, 4, 4] time(s). (9 [9, 9, 9, 9, 9, 9] picots, 8 [8, 8, 8, 8, 8, 8] shells at end of last row)

Row 7 [9, 9, 11, 11, 13, 13]: Ch 6, *sc in next shell, ch 3, dc in ch-3 sp of next picot, ch 3, rep from * across to last picot, dc in ch-3 sp of last picot, fasten off. (16 ch-3 sps)

American School of Needlework • Berne, Indiana 46711 • DRGnetwork.com

Left Front

Row 1 (WS): Ch 63, sc in 10th ch from hook *(beg 9 sk chs count as dc and ch-3 sp)*, *ch 3, sc in next ch, ch 3, sk next 2 chs, dc in next ch**, ch 3, sk next 2 chs, sc in next ch, rep from * across, ending last rep at **, turn. *(24 ch-3 sps, 16 sc, 9 dc)*

Row 2 (RS): Beg picot in first dc, *shell in ch-3 sp of next picot, picot in next dc, rep from * across to beg 9 sk chs, sk next 3 chs, ending picot in next ch, turn, leaving rem chs unworked. *(8 shells, 9 picots)*

Row 3: Ch 13, sc in 10th ch from hook, ch 3, sc in next ch, sk next 2 chs, *ch 3, dc in ch-3 sp of next picot, ch 3, picot in 3rd dc of next shell, rep from * across to last picot, dc in ch-3 sp of last picot, turn. *(8 picots, 19 ch-3 sps, 2 sc, 2 dc)*

Row 4: Beg picot in first dc, *shell in ch-3 sp of next picot, picot in next dc, rep from * across to 3 sc, ch 3, sk next sc, shell in next ch-3 sp, ch 3, sk next sc, sk next 3 chs of beg 9 sk chs, ending picot in next ch, turn. *(9 shells, 10 picots)*

Medium, Large, X-Large, 2X-Large, 3X-Large and 4X-Large Sizes Only

Rows [5 & 6, 5 & 6, 5–8, 5–8, 5–10, 5–10]: [Rep rows 3 and 4 alternately] [1, 1, 2, 2, 3, 3] time(s). *([10, 10, 11, 11, 12, 12] shells, [11, 11, 12, 12, 13, 13] picots at end of last row)*

All Sizes

Row 5 [7, 7, 9, 9, 11, 11]: Rep row 3. *(10 [11, 11, 12, 12, 13, 13] picots, 20 [22, 22, 24, 24, 26, 26] ch-3 sps, 2 sc, 2 dc)*

Row 6 [8, 8, 10, 10, 12, 12]: Beg picot in first dc, *shell in ch-3 sp of next picot, picot in next dc, rep from * across to last dc, ending picot in last dc, ch 34 [34, 41, 41, 41, 41, 41], picot in first dc of Back, [ch 3, dc in ch-3 sp of next picot, ch 3, picot in next dc] 3 [3, 4, 4, 5, 5, 5] times, *shell

in ch-3 sp of next picot, picot in next dc, rep from * across to last dc, ending picot in last dc, turn. *(20 [22, 22, 24, 24, 26, 26] shells, 28 [30, 30, 32, 34, 36, 36] picots, 12 [12, 12, 12, 16, 16, 16] ch-3 sps)*

Left Body

Row 1: Ch 6, [picot in 3rd dc of next shell, ch 3, dc in ch-3 sp of next picot, ch 3] 10 [11, 11, 12, 12, 13, 13] times, [picot in next dc, ch 3, dc in ch-3 sp of next picot, ch 3] 3 [3, 3, 3, 4, 4, 4] times, *◊[sk next 2 chs, sc in next ch, ch 3] twice, sk next 2 chs◊, dc in next ch, ch 3, rep from * 3 [3, 4, 4, 4, 4 times, rep between ◊◊ once, **dc in ch-3 sp of next picot, ch 3, picot in 3rd dc of next shell, ch 3, rep from ** across to last picot, dc in last picot, turn. *(28 [30, 31, 33, 34, 36, 36] picots, 56 [60, 62, 66, 68, 72, 72] ch-3 sps)*

Row 2: Beg picot in first dc, [shell in ch-3 sp of next picot, picot in next dc] 10 [11, 11, 12, 12, 13, 13] times, [ch 3, dc in ch-3 sp of next picot, ch 3, picot in next dc] 8 [8, 9, 9, 10, 10, 10] times, *shell in ch-3 sp of next picot, picot in next dc, rep from * across to last dc, ending picot in last dc, turn. *(20 [22, 22, 24, 24, 26, 26] shells, 29 [31, 32, 34, 35, 37, 37] picots, 12 [16, 18, 18, 20, 20, 20] ch-3 sps)*

Row 3: Ch 6, [picot in 3rd dc of next shell, ch 3, dc in ch-3 sp of next picot, ch 3] 10 [11, 11, 12, 12, 13, 13] times, [picot in next dc, ch 3, dc in ch-3 sp of next picot, ch 3] 8 [8, 9, 9, 10, 10, 10] times, *picot in 3rd dc of next shell, ch 3, dc in ch-3 sp of next picot, ch 3, rep from * across to last picot, dc in ch-3 sp of last picot, turn.

Rows 4–15 [4–15, 4–15, 4–17, 4–19, 4–19, 4–19]: [Rep rows 2 and 3 alternately] 6 [6, 6, 7, 8, 8, 8] times. At end of last row, fasten off.

Left Sleeve

Row 1: Hold piece with RS facing, sk 21 ch-3 sps on Front, join yarn

with sl st in ch-3 sp of next picot, ch 6, [picot in next dc, ch 3, dc in ch-3 sp of next picot, ch 3] 8 [8, 9, 9, 10, 10, 10] times, picot in next dc, ch 3, dc in ch-3 sp of next picot, turn. *9 [9, 10, 10, 11, 11, 11] picots, 18 [18, 20, 20, 22, 22, 22] ch-3 sps)*

Row 2: Beg picot in first dc, *ch 3, dc in ch-3 sp of next picot, ch 3, picot in next dc, rep from * across to last dc, ending picot in last dc, turn. *(10 [10, 11, 11, 12, 12, 12] picots, 18 [18, 20, 20, 22, 22, 22] ch-3 sps)*

Row 3: Ch 6, *picot in next dc, ch 3, dc in ch-3 sp of next picot, ch 3, rep from * across to last picot, dc in ch-3 sp of last picot, turn. *(9 [9, 10, 10, 11, 11, 11] picots, 18 [18, 20, 20, 22, 22, 22] ch-3 sps)*

Rows 4–7 [4–9, 4–9, 4–11, 4–11, 4–13, 4–13]: [Rep rows 2 and 3 alternately] 2 [3, 3, 4, 4, 5, 5] times.

Row 8 [10, 10, 12, 12, 14, 14]: *Ch 3, dc in ch-3 sp of next picot, ch 3, picot in next dc, rep from * across to last picot, dc in ch-3 sp of last picot, dc in last dc, turn. *(8 [8, 9, 9, 10, 10, 10] picots, 16 [16, 18, 18, 20, 20, 20] ch-3 sps)*

Rows 9–14 [11–16, 11–16, 13–18, 13–18, 15–20, 15–20]: [Rep rows 2 and 3 alternately] 3 times. *(8 [8, 9, 9, 10, 10, 10] picots, 16 [16, 18, 18, 20, 20, 20] ch-3 sps at end of last row.)*

Row 15 [17, 17, 19, 19, 21, 21]: Rep row 8 [10, 10, 12, 12, 14, 14]. *(7 [7, 8, 8, 9, 9, 9] picots, 14 [14, 16, 16, 18, 18, 18] ch-3 sps)*

Rows 16–21 [18–23, 18–23, 20–25, 20–25, 22–27, 22–27]: [Rep rows 2 and 3 alternately] 3 times.

Row 22 [24, 24, 26, 26, 28, 28]: Rep row 8 [10, 10, 12, 12, 14, 14]. *(6 [6, 7, 7, 8, 8, 8] picots, 12 [12, 14, 14, 16, 16, 16] ch-3 sps)*

Rows 23–26 [25–28, 25–30, 27–32, 27–30, 29–32, 29–32]: [Rep rows 2 and 3 alternately] 2 [2, 3, 3, 2, 2, 2] time(s). At end of last row, fasten off.

Assembly

Fold Left Sleeve in half with WS tog. Hold folded Sleeve with foundation ch to right, join yarn with sl st in first row of top piece, working in ends of rows, ch 2, sl st in first row of back half of Sleeve, ch 2, sl st in next row of back half of Sleeve, *ch 3, sk next row of front half of Sleeve, sl st in next row of front half of Sleeve, ch 3, sk next row of back half of Sleeve, sl st in next row of back half of Sleeve, rep from * across to Body, ch 3, sl st in next picot of Left Front, ch 3, sl st in next picot of Back, ch 3, sl st in next ch-3 sp of Left Front, **ch 2, sl st in next dc of Back, ch 1, sl st in next dc of Left Front***, ch 1, sl st in same dc of Back, ch 2, sl st in next ch-3 sp of Left Front, ch 1, sc in next picot of Back, ch 1, sl st in next picot of Left Front, ch 1, sc in same picot of Back, ch 1, sl st in next ch-3 sp of Left Front, rep from **across, ending last rep at ***, fasten off.

Fold Right Sleeve in half with WS tog. Hold folded Sleeve with foundation ch to right, join yarn with sl st in first row of front piece, working in ends of rows, ch 2, sl st in first row of back half of Sleeve, ch 2, sl st in next row of front half of Sleeve, *ch 3, sk next row of back half of Sleeve, sl st in next row of front half of Sleeve, ch 3, sk next row of front half of Sleeve, sl st in next row of front half of Sleeve, rep from * across to Body, now working on opposite side of foundation ch, ch 3, sl st in next picot of Back, ch 3, sl st in next picot of Right Front, ch 3, sl st in next ch-2 sp of Back, **ch 2, sl st in next dc of Right Front, ch 1, sl st in next dc of Back***, ch 1, sl st in same dc of Right Front, ch 2, sl st in next ch-2 sp of Back, ch 1, sc in next picot of Right Front, ch 1, sl st in next picot of Back, ch 1, sc in same picot of Right Front, ch 1, sl st in next ch-2 sp of Back, rep from **across, ending last rep at ***, fasten off.

Edgings
Outer Edging

Hold piece with RS facing and Right Front edge at top, join yarn with sl st in first sc in right-hand corner, ch 1, picot in same sc, sc in next ch sp, working across Right Front edge, Back neck edge, Left Front edge, and lower edge, picot in each picot and each dc, sc in each ch sp around to first sc, sl st in first sc, fasten off.

Sleeve Edging

Hold piece with RS of 1 Sleeve facing, join yarn with sl st in ch-2 sp of joining row, ch 1, sc in same sp, *picot in next picot, sc in next ch sp, picot in next dc, sc in next ch sp, rep from * around, sl st in first sc, fasten off. Rep on other Sleeve.

Drawstring

With 2 strands of yarn held tog, ch 180 [200, 220, 240, 260, 280, 300], fasten off. Weave in ends.

Finishing

Beg in 8th shell of last shell row of either Front, weave Drawstring through ch-3 sps. ∎

Honeycomb Lattice Topper

Skill Level

◼◼◼◻ INTERMEDIATE

Finished Sizes

Instructions given fit 32–34-inch
    bust *(small)*; changes for
    36–38-inch *(medium)*, 40–42-inch
    bust *(large)*, 44–46-inch bust
    (X-large), 48–50-inch bust
    (2X-large), 52–54-inch bust
    (3X-large), and 56–58-inch bust
    (4X-large) are in [ ].

Finished Garment Measurements

Bust: 36 inches *(small)* [40 inches
    (medium), 44 inches *(large)*,
    48 inches *(X-large)*, 52 inches
    (2X-large), 56 inches *(3X-large)*,
    60 inches *(4X-large)*]

Materials

• Bernat Cool Crochet light
  (light worsted) weight
  yarn (1¾ oz/200 yds/50g
  per ball):
    7 [8, 9, 9, 10, 10, 11] balls #74009
    Neapolitan shades
• Size F/5/3.75mm crochet hook or
  size needed to obtain gauge
• Tapestry needle

3 LIGHT

Gauge

[Sc in next ch-3 sp, ch 3] twice = 1
    inch; 3 rows = 1¼ inches

Pattern Notes

Weave in ends as work progresses.
Join rounds with a slip stitch unless
    otherwise stated.

Chain-4 at beginning of double crochet rows counts as first double crochet and chain-1 space unless otherwise stated.

Chain-5 at beginning of double crochet rows counts as first double crochet and chain-2 space unless otherwise stated.

Chain-6 at beginning of double crochet rows counts as first double crochet and chain-3 space unless otherwise stated.

Special Stitch

Extended double crochet (extended dc): Yo, insert hook in st indicated, yo, draw up lp, yo, draw through 1 lp on hook (first step), [yo, draw through 2 lps on hook] twice or yo, insert hook in first step of last extended dc made, yo draw through 1 lp on hook (first step), [yo, draw through 2 lps on hook] twice.

Instructions

Left Sleeve

Row 1 (RS): Ch 78 [96, 96, 96, 114, 114, 114], sc in 10th ch from hook, *ch 3, sc in next ch, ch 3, sk next 3 ch, dc in next ch**, ch 3, sk next 3 ch, sc in next ch, rep from * across, ending last rep at **, turn. *(24 [30, 30, 30, 36, 36, 36] ch sps)*

Row 2: *Ch 3, sc in next ch-3 sp, ch 3, dc in next ch-3 sp, ch 3, sc in next ch-3 sp, rep from * across, ch 1, hdc in 7th ch of beg ch, turn.

Row 3: Ch 6 *(see Pattern Notes)*, *[sc in next ch-3 sp, ch 3] twice, dc in next ch-3 sp**, ch 3, rep from * across, ending last rep at **, turn.

Row 4: *Ch 3, sc in next ch-3 sp, ch 3, dc in next ch-3 sp, ch 3, sc in next ch-3 sp, rep from * across to beg ch-6, ch 1, hdc in 3rd ch of beg ch-6, turn.

Rows 5–34 [5–36, 5–38, 5–38, 5–36, 5–34, 5–34]: [Rep Rows 3 and 4 alternately] 15 [16, 17, 17, 16, 15, 15] times.

Row 35 [37, 39, 39, 37, 35, 35]: Ch 5 *(see Pattern Notes)*, *sc in next ch-3 sp, ch 3, sc in next ch-3 sp, ch 2, dc in next ch-3 sp**, ch 2, rep from * across, ending last rep at **, turn.

Row 36 [38, 40, 40, 38, 36, 36]: Ch 3, *sc in next ch-2 sp, ch 2, dc in next ch-3 sp, [ch 2, sc in next ch-2 sp**] twice, rep from * across, ending last rep at **, ch 1, hdc in 3rd ch of beg ch-5, turn.

Row 37 [39, 41, 41, 39, 37, 37]: Ch 5, dc in ch-1 sp, *[ch 2, sc in next ch-2 sp] twice, ch 2**, dc in next ch-2 sp, rep from * across, ending last rep at **, (dc, ch 2, dc) in next ch-3 sp, turn. *(28 [32, 32, 32, 38, 38, 38] ch sps)*

Row 38 [40, 42, 42, 40, 38, 38]: Ch 3, *[sc in next ch-2 sp, ch 2**] twice, dc in next ch-2 sp, ch 2, rep from * across, ending last rep at **, sc in last ch sp, ch 1, hdc in 3rd ch of beg ch-5, turn. *(29 [33, 33, 33, 39, 39, 39] ch sps)*

Row 39 [41, 43, 43, 41, 39, 39]: Ch 3, sc in next ch-1 sp, *ch 2, dc in next ch-2 sp, [ch 2**, sc in next ch-2 sp] twice, rep from * across, ending last rep at **, (sc, ch 1, hdc) in next ch-3 sp, turn. *(28 [32, 32, 32, 38, 38, 38] ch sps)*

Row 40 [42, 44, 44, 42, 40, 40]: Ch 5, sk next ch-1 sp, *[sc in next ch-2 sp, ch 2] twice**, dc in next ch-2 sp, ch 2, rep from * across, ending last rep at **, dc in next ch-3 sp, turn. *(29 [33, 33, 33, 39, 39, 39] ch sps)*

Row 41 [43, 45, 45, 43, 41, 41]: Ch 3, *sc in next ch-2 sp, ch 2, dc in next ch-2 sp, ch 2, sc in next ch-2 sp**, ch 2, rep from * across, ch 1, hdc in 3rd ch of beg ch-5, turn.

Next rows: [Rep last 5 rows consecutively] 3 times. *(38 [42, 42, 42, 48, 48, 48] ch sps)*

Next row: Ch 5, sk ch-1 sp, *[sc in next ch-2 sp, ch 2] twice**, dc in next ch-2 sp, ch 2, rep from * across, ending last rep at **, dc in next ch-3 sp, turn. *(29 [33, 33,*

33, 39, 39, 39] ch sps)

Next row: Ch 3, *sc in next ch-2 sp, ch 2, dc in next ch-2 sp, ch 2, sc in next ch-2 sp**, ch 2, rep from * across, ch 1, hdc in 3rd ch of beg ch-5, turn.

Next row: Ch 1, sc in next ch-1 sp, *ch 5, sc in next ch-2 sp, rep from * across, sc in next ch-3 sp, fasten off.

Body

Row 1: Ch 110 [110, 116, 116, 122, 122, 122], dc in first sc on WS of Sleeve, *ch 2, sc in next ch-5 sp, rep from * across, dc in last sc, ch 111 [111, 111, 117, 117, 123, 123, 123], turn.

Row 2: Sc in 2nd ch from hook, *◊ch 2, sk 2 ch, sc in next ch◊, rep from * across to last ch, ch 2, sk last ch, sk next dc, **sc in next ch-2 sp, rep from ** across to last dc, sk last dc, sk next ch, sc in next ch, rep between ◊◊ across, turn. *(116 [116, 118, 118, 120, 120, 120] ch-2 sps)*

Row 3: *Ch 5, sc in next ch-2 sp, rep from * across to last sc, ch 2, dc in last sc, turn.

Row 4: Ch 1, sc in first dc, *ch 2, sc in next ch-5 sp, rep from * across to beg ch-5, ch 2, sc in 3rd ch of beg ch-5, turn.

Row 5: Ch 1, sc in first sc, ch 1, *sc in next ch-2 sp, ch 2, rep from * across to last sc, ch 1, sc in last sc, turn.

Row 6: Ch 1, sc in first sc, *ch 5, sc in next ch-2 sp, rep from * across to last ch-1 sp, sk last ch-1 sp, sc in last sc, turn.

Row 7: Ch 4, *sc in next ch-5 sp, ch 2, rep from * across to last sc, ch 1, dc in last sc, turn.

Row 8: Ch 1, sc in first dc, *ch 2, sc in next ch-2 sp, rep from * across to beg ch-4, ch 2, sc in 3rd ch of ch-4, turn.

Rows 9–26 [9–32, 9–38, 9–44, 9–50, 9–56, 9–62]: [Rep rows 3–8 consecutively] 3 [4, 5, 6, 7, 8, 9] times.

Left Front

Row 1: [Ch 5, sc in next ch-2 sp] 41 [41, 43, 43, 45, 45, 45] times, ch 3, sc in next ch-2 sp, ch 2, sc in next ch-2 sp, ch 1, sc in next ch-2 sp, turn. *(44 [44, 46, 46, 48, 48, 48] ch sps)*

Row 2: Sk next ch-1 sp, *ch 2, sc in next ch sp, rep from * across to beg ch-5, ch 2, sc in 3rd ch of ch-5, turn.

Row 3: Ch 1, sc in first sc, ch 1, [sc in next ch-2 sp, ch 2] 37 times, sc in next ch-2 sp, ch 1, sc in next ch-2 sp, turn. *(40 [40, 42, 42, 44, 44, 44] ch sps)*

Row 4: Ch 2, sk next ch-1 sp, sc in next ch-2 sp, ch 3, sc in next ch-2 sp, *ch 5, sc in next ch-2 sp, rep from * across to last ch-1 sp, sk last ch-1 sp, sc in last sc, turn. *(38 [38, 40, 40, 42, 42, 42] ch sps)*

Row 5: Ch 4, *sc in next ch-5 sp, ch 2, rep from * across, ch 1, sc in ch-3 sp, turn. *(37 [37, 39, 39, 41, 41, 41] ch sps)*

Row 6: Sk next ch-1 sp, *ch 2, sc in next ch-2 sp, rep from * across to beg ch-4, ch 2, sc in 3rd ch of ch-4, turn.

Row 7: [Ch 5, sc in next ch-2 sp] 33 times, ch 3, sc in next ch-2 sp, ch 2, sc in next ch-2 sp, ch 1, sc in next ch-2 sp, turn. *(36 [36, 38, 38, 40, 40, 40] ch sps)*

Row 8: Rep row 2. *(34 [34, 36, 36, 38, 38, 38] ch sps)*

Row 9: Ch 1, sc in first sc, ch 1, [sc in next ch-2 sp, ch 2] 29 [29, 31, 31, 33, 33, 33] times, sc in next ch-2 sp, ch 1, sc in next ch-2 sp, turn. *(32 [32, 34, 34, 36, 36, 36] ch sps)*

Rows 10–12: Rep rows 4–6. At end of last row, fasten off. *(28 [28, 30, 30, 32, 32, 32] ch sps)*

Back

Row 1: Hold piece with RS of Body facing, on last row of Body, sk 16 ch-2 sps from last ch-2 sp worked for Left Front, join yarn with sl st in next ch-2 sp, *ch 5, sc in next ch-2 sp, rep from * across to last sc, ch 2, dc in last sc, turn.

Rows 2–6: Rep rows 4–8 of Body.

Rows 7–48: [Rep rows 3–8 of Body consecutively] 7 times.

Row 49: Rep row 3 of Body. Fasten off.

Right Front

Row 1 (RS): Ch 86 [86, 104, 104, 122, 122, 122], sc in 2nd ch from hook, ch 2, sk next 2 chs, sc in next ch, rep from * across, turn. *(28 [28, 34, 34, 40, 40, 40] ch sps)*

Row 2: [Ch 5, sc in next ch-2 sp] 27 times, ch 3, sc in next ch-2 sp, ch 2, (sc, ch 2, dc) in last sc, turn. *(30 [30, 36, 36, 42, 42, 42] ch sps)*

Row 3: Ch 2, sc in 2nd ch from hook, *ch 2, sc in next ch sp, rep from * across to last ch-5 sp, ch 2, sc in 3rd ch of last ch-5 sp, turn.

Row 4: Ch 1, sc in first sc, ch 1, *sc in next ch-2 sp, ch 2, rep from * across to last sc, ch 2, (sc, ch 2, dc) in last sc, turn. *(31 [31, 37, 37, 43, 43, 43] ch sps)*

Row 5: Ch 9, sc in 2nd ch from hook, [ch 2, sk next ch, sc in next ch] twice, ch 3, sc in next ch-2 sp, *ch 5, sc in next ch-2 sp, rep from * across to last ch-1 sp, sk last ch-1 sp, sc in last sc, turn. *(34 [34, 40, 40, 46, 46, 46] ch sps)*

Row 6: Ch 4, *sc in next ch sp, ch 2, rep from * across to last sc, (sc, ch 2, dc) in last sc, turn. *(36 [36, 42, 42, 48, 48, 48] ch sps)*

Row 7: Ch 6, sc in 2nd ch from hook, ch 2, sk next 2 chs, sc in next ch, *ch 2, sc in next ch-2 sp, rep from * across to beg ch-4, ch 2, sc in 3rd ch of ch-4, turn. *(37 [37, 43, 43, 49, 49, 49] ch sps)*

Row 8: [Ch 5, sc in next ch-2 sp] 36 [36, 42, 42, 49, 49, 49] times, ch 3, sc in next ch-2 sp, (sc, ch 2, dc) in last sc, turn. *(39 [39, 45, 45, 51, 51, 51] ch sps)*

Row 9: Ch 9, sc in 2nd ch from hook, [ch 2, sk next ch, sc in next ch] twice, *ch 2, sc in next ch sp, rep from * across to beg ch-5, ch 2, sc in 3rd ch of ch-5, turn. *(41 [41, 47, 47, 53, 53, 53] ch sps)*

Row 10: Ch 1, sc in first sc, ch 1, *sc in next ch-2 sp, ch 2, rep from * across to last sc, ch 2, dc in last sc, turn. *(42 [42, 48, 48, 54, 54, 54] ch sps)*

Row 11: Ch 3, sc in 2nd ch from hook, ch 2, sc in next ch-2 sp, *ch 5, sc in next ch-2 sp, rep from * across to last ch-1 sp, sk last ch-1 sp, sc in last sc, turn.

Joining to Body

Row 1: Ch 4 *(see Pattern Notes)*, *sc in next ch-5 sp, ch 2, rep from * across**, ch 2, dc in last sc, ch 51, dc in first sc of Back at top, ch 2, rep from * to **, ch 1, dc in last sc, turn.

Row 2: Ch 1, sc in first dc, ◊*ch 2, sc in next ch-2 sp◊, rep from * across to ch, ch 2, sk next dc and ch, **sc in next ch, ch 2, rep from ** across to last ch, sk last ch, sk next dc, sc in next ch-2 sp, rep between ◊◊, ch 2, sc in 3rd ch of beg ch-4, turn. *(115 [115, 121, 121, 127, 127, 127] ch sps)*

Row 3: *Ch 5, sc in next ch-2 sp, rep from * across to last sc, ch 2, dc in last sc, turn.

Row 4: Ch 1, sc in first dc, *ch 2, sc in next ch-5 sp, rep from * across to beg ch-5, ch 2, sc in 3rd ch of ch-5, turn.

Row 5: Ch 1, sc in first sc, ch 1, *sc in next ch-2 sp, ch 2, rep from * across to last sc, ch 1, sc in last sc, turn.

Row 6: Ch 1, sc in first sc, *ch 5, sc in next ch-2 sp, rep from * across to last ch-1 sp, sk last ch-1 sp, sc in last sc, turn.

Row 7: Ch 4, *sc in next ch-5 sp, ch 2, rep from * across to last sc, ch 1, dc in last sc, turn.

Row 8: Ch 1, sc in first dc, *ch 2, sc in next ch-2 sp, rep from * across to beg ch-4, ch 2, sc in 3rd ch of ch-4, turn.

Rows 9–32: [Rep rows 3–8 consecutively] 4 times.

Right Sleeve

Row 1: Hold piece with WS facing, sk next 36 ch-2 sps on Front, join yarn with sl st in next ch-2 sp, *ch 5, sc in next ch-2 sp, rep from * across, ch 2, dc in next ch-2 sp, turn. *(38 [42, 42, 42, 48, 48, 48] ch sps)*

    American School of Needlework • Berne, Indiana 46711 • DRGnetwork.com

Row 2: Ch 3, sc in next ch-2 sp, *ch 2, dc in next ch-5 sp, [ch 2, sc in next ch-2 sp] twice, rep from * across to beg ch-5, ch 1, hdc in 3rd ch of beg ch-5, turn.

Row 3: Ch 5, sc in next ch-1 sp, *ch 2, sc in next ch-2 sp, ch 2**, dc in next ch-2 sp, ch 2, sc in next ch-2 sp, rep from * across, ending last rep at **, dc in next ch-3 sp, turn.

Row 4: Ch 3, sc in first ch-2 sp, *ch 2, dc in next ch-2 sp, [ch 2, sc in next ch-2 sp] twice, rep from * across to beg ch-5, ch 1, hdc in 3rd ch of beg ch-5, turn.

Row 5: Ch 5, sc in next ch-1 sp, *ch 2, sc in next ch-2 sp, ch 2**, dc in next ch-2 sp, ch 2, sc in next ch-2 sp, rep from * across, ending last rep at **, dc in next ch-3 sp, turn.

Row 6: Ch 3, sk first ch-2 sp, *dc in next ch-2 sp**, [ch 2, sc in next ch-2 sp] twice, ch 2, rep from * across, ending last rep at **, dc in 3rd ch of beg ch-5, turn. *(35 [39, 39, 39, 45, 45, 45] ch-2 sps)*

Row 7: Ch 3, *sc in next ch-2 sp, ch 2, dc in next ch-2 sp, ch 2, sc in next ch-2 sp**, ch 2, rep from * across, ending last rep at **, ch 1, hdc in 3rd ch of beg ch-3, turn. *(36 [40, 40, 40, 46, 46, 46] ch-2 sps)*

Row 8: Ch 5, sk next ch-1 sp, *[sc in next ch-2 sp, ch 2] twice, dc in next ch-2 sp, ch 2, rep from * across, dc in next ch-3 sp, turn. *(35 [39, 39, 39, 45, 45, 45] ch-2 sps)*

Rows 9–23: [Rep rows 4–8 consecutively] 3 times. *(24 [30, 30, 30, 34, 34, 34] ch-2 sps)*

Row 24: Ch 3, *sc in next ch-2 sp, ch 2, dc in next ch-2 sp, ch 2, sc in next ch-2 sp, ch 3, rep from * across, ending last rep at **, ch 1, hdc in 3rd ch of beg ch-5, turn.

Row 25: Ch 6, *[sc in next ch-3 sp, ch 3] twice, dc in next ch-3 sp**, ch 3, rep from * across, ending last rep at **, turn.

Row 26: *Ch 3, sc in next ch-3 sp, ch 3, dc in next ch-3 sp, ch 3, sc in next ch-3 sp**, rep from * across to beg ch-6, ch 1, hdc in 3rd ch of beg ch-6, turn.

Rows 27–60: [Rep rows 25 and 26 alternately] 16 [17, 18, 18, 17, 16, 16] times.

Row 61: Rep row 25. Fasten off.

Assembly

Hold piece with RS facing, fold Left Sleeve in half matching ends of rows; working in ends of rows, ch 2, sl st in 3rd ch of ch-6 at beg of same row on front half of Sleeve, *ch 2, sk next row of back half of Sleeve, sl st in next row of back half of Sleeve, ch 2, sk next row of front half of Sleeve, sl st in next row of front half of Sleeve, rep from * across to Body, **ch 2, sl st in next row of Back, ch 2, sl st in next row of Front, rep from ** across, ch 2, sl st in last row of Back, fasten off.

Hold piece with RS facing, fold Right Sleeve in half matching ends of rows; join yarn with sl st in end of first row of front half of Sleeve, ch 2, sl st in 3rd ch of ch-6 at beg of same row on back half of Sleeve, *ch 2, sk next row of front half of Sleeve, sl st in next row of front half of Sleeve, ch 2, sk next row of back half of Sleeve, sl st in next row of back half, rep from * across to Body, **ch 2, sl st in next row of Front, ch 2, sl st in next row of Back, rep from ** across, ch 2, sl st in last row of Front, turn to work along lower edge.

Edgings
Outer Edging

Rnd 1: Ch 1, sc in same st, working in ends of rows across lower edge, *ch 2, sk next row, sc in next row, rep from * across**, 3 sc in last sc, ***ch 2, sc in next ch 2 sp, rep from *** across, rep from * to **, rep from *** across, 3 sc in last sc, rep from * to **, join in first sc, ch 1, turn.

Rnd 2: *Sc in next ch-2 sp, ch 2, rep from * around, join in first sc, fasten off.

Left Sleeve Edging

Rnd 1: Hold Left Sleeve with RS facing, join yarn with sl st in ch-2 sp of joining row, ch 1, sc in same sp, *ch 2, sc in next ch-3 sp, ch 2, sc in same ch-2 sp, ch 2, sc between next 2 sc, rep from * around, join in first sc, turn.

Rnd 2: Ch 1, *sc in next ch-2 sp, ch 2, rep from * around, join in first sc, fasten off.

Right Sleeve Edging

Rnd 1: Hold Right Sleeve with RS facing, join yarn with sl st in ch-2 sp of joining row, ch 1, sc in same sp, [*ch 2, sc in next ch-3 sp, ch 2, sc in same ch-3 sp] twice, ch 2, sc in next ch-3 sp, rep from * around, join in first sc, turn.

Rnd 2: Ch 1, *sc in next ch-2 sp, ch 2, rep from * around, join in first sc, fasten off.

Drawstring

Ch 3, **extended dc** *(see Special Stitch)* in 3rd ch from hook, [extended dc in previous extended dc] 230 [250, 270, 290, 310, 330, 350] times, fasten off. Weave in ends.

Finishing

Beg in row 12 of Left Front, weave Drawstring through corresponding ch-2 sp of rows of Left Front, Back and Right Front. ■

Tropical Tank

Skill Level
■■□□ EASY

Finished Sizes
Tank: Instructions given fit 32–34-inch bust *(small)*; changes for 36–38-inch *(medium)*, 40–42-inch bust *(large)*, 44–46-inch bust *(X-large)*, 48–50-inch bust *(2X-large)*, 52–54-inch bust *(3X-large)*, and 56–58-inch bust *(4X-large)* are in [ ].
Belt: One size

Finished Garment Measurements
Tank: Bust: 34¼ inches *(small)* [38¾ inches *(medium)*, 43½ inches *(large)*, 48 inches *(X-large)*, 52½ inches *(2X-large)*, 57¼ inches *(3X-large)*, 61¾ inches *(4X-large)*]
Belt: 3 x 48 inches *(small)* [52 inches *(medium)*, 56 inches *(large)*, 59 inches *(X-large)*, 63 inches *(2X-large)*, 66 inches *(3X-large)*, 70 inches *(4X-large)*]

Materials
- Bernat Handicrafter Cotton medium (worsted) weight yarn (12 oz/608 yds/340g per ball): 4 MEDIUM
  1 [1, 2, 2, 2, 2, 2] ball(s) #33739 over the rainbow
  1 [1, 2, 2, 2, 2, 2] ball(s) #805 natural
  1 [1, 1, 1, 1, 1, 1] ball #332 tan
- Size H/8/5mm crochet hook or size needed to obtain gauge
- Tapestry needle

Gauge
4 dc = 1 inch; 8 rows = 4 inches

Pattern Notes
Weave in ends as work progresses.
Chain-3 at beginning of double crochet rows counts as first double crochet unless otherwise stated.
Chain-5 at beginning of double crochet rows counts as first double crochet and chain-2 space unless otherwise stated.

Special Stitches
Extended double crochet (extended dc): Yo, insert hook in st indicated, yo, draw up lp, yo, draw through 1 lp on hook *(first step)*, [yo, draw through 2 lps on hook] twice **or** yo, insert hook in first step of last extended dc made, yo draw through 1 lp on hook *(first step)*, [yo, draw through 2 lps on hook] twice.
Beginning V-stitch (beg V-st): (Ch 5, dc) in indicated st.
V-stitch (V-st): (Dc, ch 2, dc) in indicated st.

Instructions

Tank
Right Side Panel
Row 1 (WS): Ch 51 [51, 51, 57, 57, 57, 57], dc in 4th ch from hook *(beg 3 sk chs count as a dc)* and in next ch, *ch 2, sk next 2 chs, dc in each of next 4 chs, rep from * across to last 4 chs, ch 2, sk next 2 chs, dc in each of last 2 chs, turn. *(32 [32, 32, 36, 36, 36, 36] dc, 8 [8, 8, 9, 9, 9, 9] ch sps)*

Row 2 (RS): Ch 5 *(see Pattern Notes)*, *sc in next ch-2 sp, ch 2, sk next dc, dc in each of next 2 dc, ch 2, rep from * across to last ch-2 sp, sc in last ch-2 sp, ch 2, sk next dc, dc in last dc, turn. *(16 [16, 16, 18, 18, 18, 18] dc, 15 [15, 15, 17, 17, 17, 17] ch-2 sps, 8 [8, 8, 9, 9, 9, 9] sc)*

Row 3: Ch 3 *(see Pattern Notes)*, sk next ch-2 sp, dc in next dc, **V-st** *(see Special Stitches)* in next dc and in each rem dc across, turn. *(14 [14, 14, 16, 16, 16, 16] V-sts, 2 dc)*

Row 4: Beg V-st *(see Special Stitches)* in first dc, *sk next 2 ch-2 sps, V-st in each of next 2 dc, rep from * across to last 2 dc, dc in next dc, ch 2, dc in last dc, turn. *(13 [13, 13, 15, 15, 15, 15] V-sts)*

Row 5: Ch 3, dc in next ch-2 sp, *ch 2, dc in next ch-2 sp, dc in each of next 2 dc, dc in next ch-2 sp, rep from * across to last ch-2 sp, dc in last ch-2 sp, dc in last dc, turn. *(28 [28, 28, 32, 32, 32, 32] dc, 7 [7, 7, 8, 8, 8, 8] ch sps)*

Small Size Only
Row 6: Ch 5, *sc in next ch-2 sp, ch 2, sk next dc, dc in each of next 2 dc, ch 2, rep from * across to last ch-2 sp, sc in last ch-2 sp, ch 2, dc in last dc, turn. *(14 dc, 14 ch sps, 7 sc)*

Row 7: Ch 4, V-st in first dc and in each rem dc across, turn. *(14 V-sts)*

Row 8: Beg V-st in first dc, *sk next 2 ch-2 sps, V-st in each of next 2 dc, rep from * across to last 2 ch-2 sps, sk last 2 ch-2 sps, V-st in next dc, V-st in 4th ch of beg ch-4, turn. *(15 [15, 15, 17, 17, 17, 17] V-sts)*

Row 9: Ch 3, dc in first dc, *ch 2, dc in next ch-2 sp, dc in each of next 2 dc, dc in next ch-2 sp, rep from * across to last ch-2 sp, ch 2, dc in

last ch-2 sp, dc in last dc, turn. *(32 dc, 8 ch sps)*

Medium Size Only

Row [6]: Ch 3, dc in next dc, *2 dc in next ch-2 sp, dc in each of next 4 dc, rep from * across, turn. *([42] dc)*

Row [7]: Ch 3, sk first dc, dc in next dc, *ch 2, sk next 2 dc, dc in each of next 4 dc, rep from * across to last 2 dc, dc in each of last 2 dc, turn. *([28] dc, [7] ch sps)*

Row [8]: Ch 5, *sc in next ch-2 sp, ch 2, sk next dc, dc in each of next 2 dc, ch 2, rep from * across to last ch-2 sp, sc in last ch-2 sp, ch 2, dc in last dc, turn. *([14] dc, [14] ch sps, [7] sc)*

Row [9]: Ch 4, V-st in first dc and in each rem dc across, turn. *([14] V-sts)*

Row [10]: Beg V-st in first dc, *sk next 2 ch-2 sps, V-st in each of next 2 dc, rep from * across to last 2 ch-2 sps, sk last 2 ch-2 sps, V-st in next dc, V-st in 4th ch of beg ch-4, turn. *([15] V-sts)*

Row [11]: Ch 3, dc in first dc, *ch 2, dc in next ch-2 sp, dc in each of next 2 dc, dc in next ch-2 sp, rep from * across to last ch-2 sp, dc in last ch-2 sp, dc in last dc, turn. *([32] dc, [8] ch sps)*

Large & X-Large Sizes Only

Row [6]: Ch 3, dc in next dc, *2 dc in next ch-2 sp, dc in each of next 4 dc, rep from * across, turn. *([42, 48] dc)*

Row [7]: Ch 3, sk first dc, dc in next dc, *ch 2, sk next 2 dc, dc in each of next 4 dc, rep from * across to last 2 dc, dc in each of last 2 dc, turn. *([28, 32] dc, [7, 8] ch sps)*

Rows [8 & 9]: Rep rows [6 and 7].

Row [10]: Ch 5, *sc in next ch-2 sp, ch 2, sk next dc, dc in each of next 2 dc, ch 2, rep from * across, sc in last ch-2 sp, ch 2, dc in last dc, turn. *([14, 16] dc, [14, 16] ch sps, 7 [7, 8] sc)*

Row [11]: Ch 4, V-st in first dc and in each rem dc across, turn. *([14, 16] V-sts)*

Row [12]: Beg V-st in first dc, *sk next 2 ch-2 sps, V-st in each of next 2 dc, rep from * across to last 2 ch-2 sps, sk last 2 ch-2 sps, V-st in next dc, V-st in 4th ch of ch-4, turn. *([15, 17] V-sts)*

Row [13]: Ch 3, dc in first dc, *ch 2, dc in next ch-2 sp, dc in each of next 2 dc, dc in next ch-2 sp, rep from * across to last ch-2 sp, dc in last ch-2 sp, dc in last dc, turn. *([32, 36] dc, [8, 9] ch sps)*

2X-Large Size Only

Row [6]: Ch 3, dc in next dc, *2 dc in next ch-2 sp, dc in each of next 4 dc, rep from * across, turn. *([48] dc)*

Row [7]: Ch 3, sk first dc, dc in next dc, *ch 2, sk next 2 dc, dc in each of next 4 dc, rep from * across to last 2 dc, dc in last 2 dc, turn. *([32] dc, [8] ch sps)*

Rows [8–11]: [Rep rows [6 and 7] alternately] twice.

Row [12]: Ch 5, *sc in next ch-2 sp, ch 2, sk next dc, dc in each of next 2 dc, ch 2, rep from * across to last ch-2 sp, sc in last ch-2 sp, ch 2, dc in last dc, turn. *([16] dc, [16] ch sps, [8] sc)*

Row [13]: Ch 4, V-st in first dc and in each rem dc across, turn. *([16] V-sts)*

Row [14]: Beg V-st in first dc, *sk next 2 ch-2 sps, V-st in each of next 2 dc, rep from * across to last 2 ch-2 sps, sk last 2 ch-2 sps, V-st in next dc, V-st in 4th ch of ch-4, turn. *([17] V-sts)*

Row [15]: Ch 3, dc in first dc, *ch 2, dc in next ch-2 sp, dc in each of next 2 dc, dc in next ch-2 sp, rep from * across to last ch-2 sp, dc in last ch-2 sp, dc in last dc, turn. *([36] dc, [9] ch sps)*

3X-Large & 4X-Large Sizes Only

Row [6]: Ch 3, dc in next dc, *2 dc in next ch-2 sp, dc in each of next 4 dc, rep from * across, turn. *([48, 48] dc)*

Row [7]: Ch 3, sk first dc, dc in next dc, *ch 2, sk next 2 dc, dc in each of next 4 dc, rep from * across to last 2 dc, dc in each of last 2 dc, turn. *([32, 32] dc, [8, 8] ch sps)*

Row [8]: Ch 5, *sc in next ch-2 sp, ch 2, sk next dc, dc in each of next 2 dc, ch 2, rep from * across to last ch-2 sp, sc in last ch-2 sp, ch 2, dc in last dc, turn. *([16, 16] dc, [16, 16] ch sps, [8, 8] sc)*

Row [9]: Beg V-st in first dc, V-st in each dc across, turn. *([16, 16] V-sts)*

Row [10]: Beg V-st in first dc, *sk next 2 ch-2 sps, V-st in each of next 2 dc, rep from * across to last dc, V-st in last dc, turn.

Rows [11 & 12, 11–16]: Rep row [10] [2, 6] times.

Rows [13–16, 17–20]: Rep rows [5–8].

Row [17, 21]: Ch 4, V-st in first dc and in each rem dc across, turn. *([16, 16] V-sts)*

Row [18, 22]: Beg V-st in first dc, *sk next 2 ch-2 sps, V-st in each of next 2 dc, rep from * across to last 2 ch-2 sps, sk last 2 ch-2 sps, V-st in next dc, V-st in 4th ch of ch-4, turn. *([17, 17] V-sts)*

Row [19, 23]: Ch 3, dc in first dc, *ch 2, dc in next ch-2 sp, dc in each of next 2 dc, dc in next ch-2 sp, rep from * across to last ch-2 sp, dc in last ch-2 sp, dc in last dc, turn. *([36, 36] dc, [9, 9] ch sps)*

Right Shoulder
For All Sizes

Note: Right Shoulder is joined to both sides of Side Panel.

Row 1: Ch 3, dc in next dc, *2 dc in next ch-2 sp, dc in each of next 4 dc, rep from * across to last dc, **extended dc** *(see Special Stitches)* in 3rd ch of ch-3, work 30 [42, 54, 42, 54, 54, 66] extended dc, work 1st step of extended dc, sl st in 1st ch of foundation row, complete extended dc, dc in next ch, **2 dc in next ch-2 sp, dc in each of next 4 ch, rep from ** to end, turn. *(126 [138, 150, 150, 162, 162, 174] dc)*

Row 2: Ch 3, dc in next dc, *ch 2, sk next 2 dc, dc in each of next 4 dc, rep from * across, dc in last 2 dc, turn. *(84 [92, 100, 100, 108, 108, 116] dc, 21 [23, 25, 25, 27, 27, 29] ch sps)*

Row 3: Ch 5, *sc in next ch-2 sp, ch 2, sk next dc, dc in each of next 2 dc, ch 2, rep from * across, sc in last ch-2 sp, ch 2, dc in last dc, turn. *(42 [46, 50, 50, 54, 54, 58] dc, 42 [46, 50, 50, 54, 54, 58] ch sps, 21 [23, 25, 25, 27, 27, 29] sc)*

Row 4: Ch 5, dc in first dc, V-st in each dc across, turn. *(42 [46, 50, 50, 54, 54, 58] V-sts)*

Row 5: Ch 5, dc in first dc, *sk next 2 ch-2 sps, V-st in each of next 2 dc, rep from * across, V-st in last dc, turn.

Small, Medium & Large Sizes Only

Row 6: Ch 3, dc in next ch-2 sp, *ch 2, dc in next ch-2 sp, dc in each of next 2 dc, dc in next ch-2 sp, rep from * across to last ch-2 sp, dc in last ch-2 sp, dc in last dc, turn. *(84 [92, 100] dc, 21 [23, 25] ch sps)*

Row 7: Ch 3, dc in next dc, *2 dc in next ch-2 sp, dc in each of next 4 dc, rep from * across, turn. *(126 [138, 150] dc)*

X-Large, 2X-Large, 3X-Large & 4X-Large Only

Rows [6 & 7]: Rep row 5 twice.

Row [8]: Ch 3, dc in next ch-2 sp, *ch 2, dc in next ch-2 sp, dc in each of next 2 dc, dc in next ch-2 sp, rep from * across to last ch-2 sp, dc in last ch-2 sp, dc in last dc, turn. *([100, 108, 108, 116] dc, [25, 27, 27, 29] ch sps)*

Row [9]: Ch 3, dc in next dc, *2 dc in next ch-2 sp, dc in each of next 4 dc, rep from * across, turn. *([150, 162, 162, 174] dc)*

Back
For All Sizes

Row 1: Ch 3, dc in next dc, [ch 2, sk next 2 dc, dc in each of next 4 dc] 8 [9, 10, 10, 11, 11, 12] times, ch 2,

sk next 2 dc, dc in each of next 2 dc, leaving rem sts unworked, turn. *(36 [40, 44, 44, 48, 48, 52] dc, 9 [10, 11, 11, 12, 12, 13] ch sps)*

Row 2: Ch 5, *sc in next ch-2 sp, ch 2, sk next dc, dc in next 2 dc, ch 2, rep from * across to last ch-2 sp, sc in last ch-2 sp, ch 2, dc in last dc, turn. *(18 [20, 22, 22, 24, 24, 26] dc, 18 [20, 22, 22, 24, 24, 26] ch sps, 9 [10, 11, 11, 12, 12, 13] sc)*

Row 3: Beg V-st in first dc, V-st in each rem dc across, turn. *(18 [20, 22, 22, 24, 24, 26] V-sts)*

Row 4: Beg V-st in first dc, *sk next 2 ch-2 sps, V-st in each of next 2 dc, rep from * across to last dc, V-st in last dc, turn.

Rows 5 & 6 [5–8, 5–10, 5–10, 5–12, 5–12, 5–12]: Rep row 4 2 [4, 6, 6, 8, 8, 8] times.

Row 7 [9, 11, 11, 13, 13, 13]: Ch 3, dc in next ch-2 sp, *ch 2, dc in next ch-2 sp, dc in each of next 2 dc, dc in next ch-2 sp, rep from * across to last ch-2 sp, dc in last ch-2 sp, dc in last dc, fasten off. *(36 [40, 44, 44, 48, 48, 52] dc, 9 [10, 11, 11, 12, 12, 13] ch sps)*

Front

Row 1: Sk next unused 24 dc on row 1 of Right Shoulder, join yarn with sl st in next dc, ch 3, dc in next dc, *ch 2, sk next 2 dc, dc in each of next 4 dc, rep from * across to last 2 dc, dc in each of last 2 dc, turn. *(32 [36, 40, 40, 44, 44, 48] dc, 8 [9, 10, 10, 11, 11, 12] ch sps)*

Row 2: Ch 5, *sc in next ch-2 sp, ch 2, sk next dc, dc in each of next 2 dc, ch 2, rep from * across to last ch-2 sp, sc in last ch-2 sp, ch 2, dc in last dc, turn. *(16 [18, 20, 20, 22, 22, 24] dc, 16 [18, 20, 20, 22, 22, 24] ch sps, 8 [9, 10, 10, 11, 11, 12] sc)*

Row 3: Beg V-st in first dc, V-st in each rem dc across, turn. *(16 [18, 20, 20, 22, 22, 24] V-sts)*

Row 4: Beg V-st in first dc, *sk next 2 ch-2 sps, V-st in each of next 2 dc, rep from * across, V-st in last dc, turn.

Rows 5 & 6 [5–8, 5–10, 5–10, 5–12, 5–12, 5–12]: Rep row 4 2 [4, 6, 6, 8, 8, 8] times.

Row 7 [9, 11, 11, 13, 13, 13]: Ch 3, dc in next ch-2 sp, *ch 2, dc in next ch-2 sp, dc in each of next 2 dc, dc in next ch-2 sp, rep from * across to last ch-2 sp, dc in last ch-2 sp, dc in last dc, turn. *(32 [36, 40, 40, 44, 44, 48] dc, 8 [9, 10, 10, 11, 11, 12] ch sps)*

Left Shoulder

Row 1: Ch 3, dc in next dc, *2 dc in next ch-2 sp, dc in each of next 4 dc, rep from * across to last dc, extended dc in last dc, work 24 extended dc, work first step of extended dc, sl st in first dc on Back, complete extended dc, dc in next dc, **2 dc in next ch-2 sp, dc in each of next 4 dc, rep from ** to end, turn. *(126 [138, 150, 150, 162, 162, 174] dc)*

Rep instructions for Right Shoulder reversing shaping.

Left Side Panel

Row 1: Ch 3, dc in next dc, [ch 2, sk next 2 dc, dc in each of next 4 dc] 7 times, ch 2, sk next 2 dc, dc in next 2 dc, turn. *(32 [32, 32, 36, 36, 36, 36] dc, 8 [8, 8, 9, 9, 9, 9] ch sps)*

Row 2: Ch 3, *sc in next ch-2 sp, ch 2, sk next dc, dc in each of next 2 dc, ch 2, rep from * across to last ch-2 sp, sc in last ch-2 sp, ch 2, dc in last dc, turn. *(16 [16, 16, 18, 18, 18, 18] dc, 15 [15, 15, 17, 17, 17, 17] ch-2 sps, 8 [8, 8, 9, 9, 9, 9] sc)*

Row 3: Beg V-st in first dc, V-st in each rem dc across to last 2, dc in next dc, tr in last dc, turn. *(14 [14, 14, 16, 16, 16, 16] V-sts, 1 dc, 1 tr)*

Row 4: Ch 5, sk tr and next dc, dc in next dc, V-st in next dc, *sk next 2 ch-2 sps, V-st in each of next 2 dc, rep from * across to last dc, V-st in last dc, turn. *(14 [14, 14, 16, 16, 16, 16] V-sts)*

Row 5: Ch 3, dc in next ch-2 sp, *ch 2, dc in next ch-2 sp, dc in each of next 2 dc, dc in next ch-2 sp, rep from * across to last ch-2 sp, dc in

last ch-2 sp, dc in last dc, turn. *(28 [28, 28, 32, 32, 32, 32] dc, 7 [7, 7, 8, 8, 8, 8] ch sps)*

Small Size Only
Row 6: Ch 5, *sc in next ch-2 sp, ch 2, sk next dc, dc in each of next 2 dc, ch 2, rep from * across to last ch-2 sp, sc in last ch-2 sp, ch 2, dc in last dc, turn. *(14 dc, 14 ch sps, 7 sc)*

Row 7: Beg V-st in first dc, V-st in each rem dc across to last dc, (V-st, tr) in last dc, turn. *(14 V-sts, 1 tr)*

Row 8: Beg V-st in first tr, V-st in next dc, *sk next 2 ch-2 sps, V-st in each of next 2 dc, rep from * across to last dc, V-st in last dc, turn. *(15 V-sts)*

Row 9: Ch 3, dc in next ch-2 sp, *ch 2, dc in next ch-2 sp, dc in each of next 2 dc, dc in next ch-2 sp, rep from * across to last ch-2 sp, dc in last ch-2 sp, ch 2, 2 dc in last dc, fasten off. *(32 dc, 8 ch sps)*

Medium Size Only
Row [6]: Ch 3, dc in next dc, *2 dc in next ch-2 sp, dc in each of next 4 dc, rep from * across, turn. *([42] dc)*

Row [7]: Ch 3, dc in next dc, *ch 2, sk next 2 dc, dc in each of next 4 dc, rep from * across to last 2 dc, dc in each of last 2 dc, turn. *([28] dc, [7] ch sps)*

Row [8]: Ch 5, *sc in next ch-2 sp, ch 2, sk next dc, dc in each of next 2 dc, ch 2, rep from * across to last ch-2 sp, sc in last ch-2 sp, ch 2, dc in last dc, turn. *([14] dc, [14] ch sps, [7] sc)*

Row [9]: Beg V-st in first dc, V-st in each rem dc across to last dc, (V-st, tr) in last dc, turn. *([14] V-sts, 1 tr)*

Row [10]: Beg V-st in first tr, V-st in next dc, *sk next 2 ch-2 sps, V-st in each of next 2 dc, rep from * across to last dc, V-st in last dc, turn. *([15] V-sts)*

Row [11]: Ch 3, dc in next ch-2 sp, *ch 2, dc in next ch-2 sp, dc in each of next 2 dc, dc in next ch-2 sp, rep from * across to last ch-2

sp, dc in last ch-2 sp, ch 2, 2 dc in last dc, fasten off. *([32] dc, [8] ch sps)*

Large & X-Large Sizes Only
Row [6]: Ch 3, dc in next dc, *2 dc in next ch-2 sp, dc in each of next 4 dc, rep from * across, turn. *([42, 48] dc)*

Row [7]: Ch 3, dc in next dc, *ch 2, sk next 2 dc, dc in each of next 4 dc, rep from * across to last 2 dc, dc in each of last 2 dc, turn. *([28, 32] dc, [7, 8] ch sps)*

Rows [8 & 9]: Rep rows [6 and 7].

Row [10]: Ch 5, *sc in next ch-2 sp, ch 2, sk next dc, dc in each of next 2 dc, ch 2, rep from * across to last ch-2 sp, sc in last ch-2 sp, ch 2, dc in last dc, turn. *([14, 16] dc, [14, 16] ch sps, [7, 8] sc)*

Row [11]: Ch 5, dc in first dc, V-st in each dc across to last dc, (V-st, tr) in last dc, turn. *([14, 16] V-sts, 1 tr)*

Row [12]: Beg V-st in first tr, V-st in next dc, *sk next 2 ch-2 sps, V-st in each of next 2 dc, rep from * across to last dc, V-st in last dc, turn. *([15, 17] V-sts)*

Row [13]: Ch 3, dc in next ch-2 sp, *ch 2, dc in next ch-2 sp, dc in each of next 2 dc, dc in next ch-2 sp, rep from * across to last ch-2 sp, dc in last ch-2 sp, ch 2, 2 dc in last dc, fasten off. *([32, 36] dc, [8, 9] ch sps)*

2X-Large Size Only
Row [6]: Ch 3, dc in next dc, *2 dc in next ch-2 sp, dc in each of next 4 dc, rep from * across, turn. *([48] dc)*

Row [7]: Ch 3, dc in next dc, *ch 2, sk next 2 dc, dc in each of next 4 dc, rep from * across to last 2 dc, dc in each of last 2 dc, turn. *([32] dc, [8] ch sps)*

Rows [8–11]: [Rep rows 6 and 7] twice.

Row [12]: Ch 5, *sc in next ch-2 sp, ch 2, sk next dc, dc in each of next 2 dc, ch 2, rep from * across to last ch-2 sp, sc in last ch-2 sp, ch 2, dc in last dc, turn. *([16] dc, [16] ch sps, [8] sc)*

Row [13]: Ch 5, dc in first dc, V-st in each dc across to last dc, (V-st, tr) in last dc, turn. *(14 [14, 14, 16, 16, 16, 16] V-sts, 1 tr)*

Row [14]: Beg V-st in first tr, V-st in next dc, *sk next 2 ch-2 sps, V-st in each of next 2 dc, rep from * across, V-st in last dc, turn. *([17] V-sts)*

Row [15]: Ch 3, dc in next ch-2 sp, *ch 2, dc in next ch-2 sp, dc in each of next 2 dc, dc in next ch-2 sp, rep from * across to last ch-2 sp, dc in last ch-2 sp, ch 2, 2 dc in last dc, fasten off. *([36] dc, [9] ch sps)*

3X-Large & 4X-Large Sizes Only
Row [6]: Ch 3, dc in next dc, *2 dc in next ch-2 sp, dc in each of next 4 dc, rep from * across, turn. *([48, 48] dc)*

Row [7]: Ch 3, dc in next dc, *ch 2, sk next 2 dc, dc in each of next 4 dc, rep from * across to last 2 dc, dc in each of last 2 dc, turn. *([32, 32] dc, [8, 8] ch sps)*

Row [8]: Ch 5, *sc in next ch-2 sp, ch 2, sk next dc, dc in each of next 2 dc, ch 2, rep from * across to last ch-2 sp, sc in last ch-2 sp, ch 2, dc in last dc, turn. *([16, 16] dc, [16, 16] ch sps, [8, 8] sc)*

Row [9]: Beg V-st in first dc, V-st in each dc across, turn. *([16, 16] V-sts)*

Row [10]: Beg V-st in first dc, *sk next 2 ch-2 sps, V-st in each of next 2 dc, rep from * across to last dc, V-st in last dc, turn.

Rows [11 & 12, 11–16]: Rep row [10] [2, 6] times.

Rows [13–16, 17–20]: Rep rows [5–8].

Row [17, 21]: Beg V-st in first dc, V-st in each dc across to last dc, (V-st, tr) in last dc, turn. *([16, 16] V-sts, 1 tr)*

Row [18, 22]: Beg V-st in first tr, V-st in next dc, *sk next 2 ch-2 sps, V-st in each of next 2 dc, rep from * across to last dc, V-st in last dc, turn. *([17, 17] V-sts)*

   American School of Needlework • Berne, Indiana 46711 • DRGnetwork.com

Row [19, 23]: Ch 3, dc in next ch-2 sp, *ch 2, dc in next ch-2 sp, dc in each of next 2 dc, dc in next ch-2 sp, rep from * across to last ch-2 sp, dc in last ch-2 sp, ch 2, 2 dc in last dc, fasten off. *([36, 36] dc, [9, 9] ch sps)*

Finishing
Matching lower edges, sew Left Side Panel to Left Shoulder Panel.

Edgings
Front Neckline Edging
Hold piece with RS of Front facing, join yarn with sl st in last unworked dc of Left Shoulder, working in ends of rows across Front, 2 sc in each row across, sl st in first unworked dc of Right Shoulder, fasten off.

Back Neckline Edging
Hold piece with RS of Back facing, join yarn with sl st in last unworked dc of Right Shoulder, working in ends of rows across Back, 2 sc in each row across, sl st in first unworked dc of Left Shoulder, fasten off.

Armhole Edging
Hold piece with RS of 1 underarm facing, join yarn with sl st in last unworked dc of shoulder, working in ends of rows around armhole, 2 sc in each row around, sl st in first unworked dc of same shoulder, fasten off. Rep for other armhole.

Lower Edging
Hold piece with RS facing and lower edge at top, join yarn with sl st in seam, working in ends of rows, 2 sc in each row around, sl st in first sc, fasten off.

Belt
Row 1: Ch 3 *(see Pattern Notes)*, **extended dc** *(see Special Stitches)* in 3rd ch from hook, work 10 extended dc, turn. *(12 dc)*

Row 2: Ch 3, dc in next dc, ch 2, sk next 2 dc, dc in each of next 4 dc, ch 2, sk next 2 dc, dc in each of next 2 dc, turn. *(8 dc, 2 ch-2 sps)*

Row 3: Ch 5 *(see Pattern Notes)*, sc in next ch-2 sp, ch 2, sk next dc, dc in each of next 2 dc, ch 2, sc in next ch-2 sp, ch 2, dc in last dc, turn. *(4 dc, 2 sc, 4 ch-2 sps)*

Row 4: Beg V-st *(see Special Stitches)* in first dc, **V-st** *(see Special Stitches)* in each dc across, turn. *(4 V-sts)*

Row 5: Beg V-st in first dc, sk next 2 ch-2 sps, V-st in each of next 2 dc, sk next 2 ch-2 sps, V-st in last dc, turn. *(4 V-sts)*

Row 6: Ch 3, dc in next ch-2 sp, ch 2, dc in next ch-2 sp, dc in each of next 2 dc, dc in next ch-2 sp, ch 2, dc in last 2 dc, turn. *(8 dc, 2 ch-2 sps)*

Row 7: Ch 3, dc in next dc, 2 dc in next ch-2 sp, dc in each of next 4 dc, 2 dc in next ch-2 sp, dc in next 2 dc, turn. *(12 dc)*

Rows 8–97 [8–104, 8–111, 8–118, 8–125, 8–132, 8–139]: [Rep rows 2–7 consecutively] 13 [14, 15, 16, 17, 18, 19] times. At end of last row, fasten off. ∎

Short & Sweet Sweater

Skill Level

■■□□ EASY

Finished Sizes

Instructions given fit 32–34-inch bust (small); changes for 36–38-inch (medium), 40–42-inch bust (large), 44–46-inch bust (X-large), 48–50-inch bust (2X-large), 52–54-inch bust (3X-large), and 56–58-inch bust (4X-large) are in [ ].

Finished Garment Measurements

Bust: 39¼ inches (small) [44¾ inches (medium), 47¼ inches (large), 50 inches (X-large), 58 inches (2X-large), 63¼ inches (3X-large), 68¾ inches (4X-large)]

Materials

- Red Heart Hula light (sport) weight yarn (3½ oz/238 yds/100g per skein):
  5 [5, 6, 6, 7, 7, 8] skeins #1934 pink
- Size H/8/5mm crochet hook or size needed to obtain gauge
- Tapestry needle

Gauge

7 sts = 2 inches; 6 rows = 2 inches

Pattern Notes

Weave in ends as work progresses.
Chain-3 at beginning of double crochet row counts as first double crochet unless otherwise stated.

Special Stitch

Extended half double crochet (extended hdc): Yo, insert hook in st indicated, yo, draw up lp, yo, draw through 1 lp on hook (first step), yo, draw through all 3 lps on hook.

Instructions

Right Sleeve

Row 1 (RS): Ch 3, **extended hdc** (see Special Stitch) in 3rd ch from hook, [extended hdc in first step of last extended hdc] 65 [69, 73, 79, 85, 91, 97] times, turn. (66 [70, 74, 80, 86, 92, 98] hdc)

Row 2: Ch 3, hdc in 3rd ch from hook, *hdc between next 2 hdc, rep from * across, hdc in sp between last hdc and beg ch, hdc in 2nd ch of beg ch-3, turn. (68 [72, 76, 82, 88, 94, 100] hdc)

Row 3: Ch 3, hdc in 3rd ch from hook, hdc in each hdc across, hdc in 2nd ch of beg beg ch-3, turn. (70 [74, 78, 84, 90, 96, 102] hdc)

Rows 4–13: [Rep rows 2 and 3 alternately] 5 times, turn. (90 [94, 98, 104, 110, 116, 122] hdc)

Row 14: Rep row 2. At end of row, fasten off. (92 [96, 100, 106, 112, 118, 124] hdc

Right Body

Row 1 (RS): Ch 3, extended hdc in 3rd ch from hook, *[extended hdc in first step of last extended hdc] 14 times**, work first step of extended hdc, sl st in last hdc of row 14 of Right Sleeve, complete extended hdc, hdc in each hdc across to beg ch-3, work first step of extended hdc in beg ch, sl st in beg ch, complete extended hdc, [extended hdc in first step of last extended hdc] 14 times, turn. (122 [126, 130, 136, 142, 148, 154] hdc)

Row 2: Ch 2, *hdc between next 2 hdc, rep from * across, ending hdc in sp between last hdc and beg ch, turn.

Row 3: Ch 2, hdc in each hdc across, turn.

Rows 4–21 [4–23, 4–25, 4–27, 4–31, 4–35, 4–39]: [Rep rows 2 and 3 alternately] 9 [10, 11, 12, 14, 16, 18] times.

Back

Row 1 (WS): [Hdc between next 2 hdc] 58 [60, 62, 65, 68, 71, 74] times, turn, leaving rem sts unworked. (58 [60, 62, 65, 68, 71, 74] hdc)

Row 2 (RS): Ch 2, hdc in each hdc across, turn.

Row 3: Ch 2, *hdc between next 2 hdc, rep from * across, hdc in sp between last hdc and beg ch, turn.

Rows 4–17 [4–21, 4–21, 4–21, 4–25, 4–25, 4–25]: [Rep rows 2 and 3 alternately] 7 [9, 9, 9, 11, 11, 11] times, fasten off.

Right Front

Row 1 (WS): Hold piece with WS of last row of Right Body facing, sk 16 [16, 18, 18, 18, 20, 22] hdc from Back, join yarn with sl st in next sp between hdc, ch 2, **hdc dec** (see Stitch Guide) in next 2 sps between hdc, *hdc between next 2 hdc, rep from * across, hdc in sp between last hdc and beg ch, turn. (47 [49, 49, 52, 55, 56, 57] hdc)

Row 2: Ch 2, hdc in each hdc across to last 4 hdc, hdc dec in next 2 hdc, ch 2, turn, leaving rem hdc unworked. (45 [47, 47, 50, 53, 54, 55] hdc)

Row 3: Sk sp between first 2 hdc, hdc dec in next 2 sps between hdc, *hdc between next 2 hdc, rep from * across, hdc in sp between last hdc and beg ch, ch 2, turn. (43 [45, 45, 48, 51, 52, 53] hdc)

Rows 4–7 [4–9, 4–9, 4–9, 4–11, 4–11, 4–11]: [Rep rows 2 and 3 alternately] 2 [3, 3, 3, 4, 4, 4] times. (35 [33, 33, 36, 35, 36, 37] hdc)

Row 8 [10, 10, 10, 12, 12, 12]: Rep row 2. At end of row, fasten off. (33 [31, 31, 34, 33, 34, 35] hdc)

Left Front

Row 1 (RS): Ch 3, extended hdc in 3rd ch from hook, [extended hdc in first step of last extended hdc] 30 [30, 30, 33, 34, 35, 36] times, turn. (33 [31, 31, 34, 35, 36, 37] hdc)

Row 2: Ch 4, hdc in 3rd ch from hook, hdc in next ch, *hdc between next 2 hdc, rep from * across, hdc in sp between last

hdc and beg ch, turn. (35 [33, 33, 36, 37, 38, 39] hdc)

Row 3: Ch 2, hdc in each hdc across, work first step of extended hdc, sl st in beg ch, complete extended hdc, extended hdc in last extended hdc, turn. (37 [35, 35, 38, 39, 40, 41] hdc)

Rows 4–7 [4–9, 4–9, 4–9, 4–11, 4–11, 4–11]: [Rep rows 2 and 3 alternately] 2 [3, 3, 3, 4, 4, 4] times. (45 [47, 47, 50, 53, 54, 55] hdc)

Row 8 [10, 10, 10, 12, 12, 12]: Rep row 2. (47 [49, 49, 52, 55, 56, 57] hdc)

Left Body

Row 1: Ch 2, *hdc in each hdc across**, work first step of extended hdc, sl st in beg ch, complete extended hdc, [extended hdc in first step of last extended hdc] 16 [16, 18, 18, 18, 20, 22] times, work first step of extended hdc, on WS of Back, sl st in ch-1 sp at end of last row, complete extended hdc, rep from * to **, ch 2, turn. (122 [126, 130, 136, 142, 148, 154] hdc)

Row 2: Ch 2, *hdc between next 2 hdc, rep from * across, ending hdc in sp between last hdc and beg ch, ch 2, turn.

Row 3: Ch 2, hdc in each hdc across, turn.

Rows 4–21 [4–23, 4–25, 4–27, 4–31, 4–35, 4–39]: [Rep rows 2 and 3 alternately] 9 [10, 11, 12, 14, 16, 18] times. At end of last row, fasten off.

Left Sleeve

Row 1 (WS): Hold piece with WS of Left Body facing, sk next 14 hdc, join yarn with sl st in next hdc, ch 2, [hdc between next 2 hdc] 92 [96, 100, 106, 112, 118,

124] times, ch 2, turn. (92 [96, 100, 106, 112, 118, 124] hdc)

Row 2: Ch 2, **hdc dec** (see Stitch Guide) in first 2 hdc, hdc in each hdc across to last 2 hdc, hdc dec in last 2 hdc, ch 2, turn. (90 [94, 98, 104, 110, 116, 122] hdc)

Row 3: Ch 2, working in sps between hdc, hdc dec in next 2 sps, *hdc between next 2 hdc, rep from * across, ending hdc dec in sp between last 2 hdc and sp between last hdc and beg ch, turn. (88 [92, 96, 102, 108, 114, 120] hdc)

Rows 4–13: [Rep rows 2 and 3 alternately] 5 times.

Row 14: Rep row 2. At end of last row, fasten off. (66 [70, 74, 80, 86, 92, 98] hdc)

Assembly

Hold Front and Back with RS tog and left side edges at top, working in ends of rows of both pieces at same time, join yarn with sl st in of end of first row of Sleeve, ch 1, sc in same sp, sc in end of each row across, fasten off. Join rem side edges in same manner.

Neck Edging

Row 1 (RS): Hold piece with RS facing, join yarn with sl st in last hdc at top of last row of Right Front, ch 1, sc in same st, *working in ends of rows, **2 sc in each row, rep from ** across *** to shoulder, (16 [20, 20, 20, 24, 24, 24] sc), ◊[hdc between next 2 hdc] 16 [16, 18, 18, 18, 20, 22] times◊, hdc in next hdc, (17 [17, 19, 19, 19, 21, 23] hdc), hdc in each row along Back neck edge, (17 [21, 21, 21, 25, 25, 25] hdc), hdc in next hdc, rep between ◊◊ once, rep from * to ***, turn. (95 sts)

Row 2: Ch 1, sk first sc, hdc in each sc, hdc between next 2 hdc, hdc in each sc, sk last sc, turn. (85 [93, 93, 93, 101, 101, 101] hdc)

Row 3: Ch 1, sc in each of first 5 sts, *hdc between next 2 hdc, rep from * across until 5 sts remain, sc in each of next 4 sts, sl st in next st, turn. (75 [83, 83, 83, 91, 91, 91] hdc, 9 sc, 1 sl st)

Row 4: Ch 1, sk first sc, sl st in each of next 2 sc, sc in each of next 2 sc, [hdc between next 2 sts] 3 times, *hdc in next hdc, hdc between same hdc and next hdc, rep from * across until 8 sts remain, [hdc between next 2 sts] 3 times, sc in each of next 2 sc, sl st in next sc, turn. (144 [160, 160, 160, 176, 176, 176] hdc, 4 sc, 3 sl sts)

Row 5: Ch 1, sk first sc, *hdc between next 2 sts, sk sp between next 2 hdc, rep from * across to last hdc, hdc between last hdc and next sc, **do not turn**. (74 [82, 82, 82, 90, 90, 90] hdc)

Edgings
Outer Edging

Sc in each of next 2 sc, ◊working in ends of rows 1–4 of Collar, sc in each row ◊, working across Left Front, *sc between next 2 hdc, rep from * to bottom, ch 2, working in ends of rows, hdc evenly spaced along lower edge to Right Front, ch 2, **sc between next 2 hdc, rep from ** to beg of Collar, rep between ◊◊ once, sl st in first hdc of row 5 of Collar, fasten off.

Sleeve Edging

Hold 1 Sleeve with RS facing, join yarn with sl st at underarm joining, ch 1, sc in same sp, *sc between next 2 hdc, rep from * around edge, sl st in beg sc, fasten off. Rep on other Sleeve. ■

Essential Shell

Skill Level

Finished Sizes

Instructions given fit 32–34-inch bust (small); changes for 36–38-inch (medium), 40–42-inch bust (large), 44–46-inch bust (X-large), 48–50-inch bust (2X-large), 52–54-inch bust (3X-large), and 56–58-inch bust (4X-large) are in [ ].

Finished Garment Measurements

Bust: 35½ inches (small) [39¼ inches (medium), 42½ inches (large), 46¼ inches (X-large), 50½ inches (2X-large), 54¼ inches (3X-large), 57¾ inches (4X-large)]

Materials

- Patons Grace light (light worsted) weight yarn (1¾ oz/136 yds/50g per ball): 6 [6, 7, 7, 8, 9, 10] balls #60008 natural
- Size G/6/4mm crochet hook or size needed to obtain gauge
- Size 7/1.65mm steel crochet hook or size needed to obtain gauge
- Tapestry needle

Gauges

Size G hook in lace pattern: 9 sts = 2 inches; 9 rows = 2 inches
Size 7 hook in front lp sc pattern: 9 sts = 1¾ inches; 9 rows = 1¾ inches

Pattern Notes

Weave in ends as work progresses. Chain-3 at beginning of double crochet row counts as first double crochet unless otherwise stated.

Pattern Stitch

Lace pattern: Sc in first st, *dc in next sc, sc in next dc, rep from * across to last st, hdc in last sc.

Special Stitches

Front loop single crochet (front lp sc): Sc in **front lp** (see Stitch Guide) in indicated st.

Picot: (Sc, ch 3, sc) in indicated st.
Shell: 5 dc in indicated sp.

Instructions

Right Side Panel

Row 1 (WS): With size 7 hook, ch 71 [73, 75, 77, 79, 79, 79], sc in 2nd ch from hook and each ch across, turn. (70 [72, 74, 76, 78, 78, 78] sc)

Row 2 (RS): Ch 1, **front lp sc** (see Special Stitches) in each sc across to last 2 sc, **sc dec** (see Stitch Guide) in last 2 sc, turn. (69 [71, 73, 75, 77, 77, 77] sc)

Row 3: Ch 1, sc dec in first 2 sc, front lp sc in each sc across, turn. (68 [70, 72, 74, 76, 76, 76] sc)

Row 4: Ch 1, front lp sc in each sc across to last 2 sc, sc dec in last 2 sc, turn. (67 [69, 71, 73, 75, 75, 75] sc)

Row 5: Ch 1, sc dec in first 2 sc, sc dec in next 2 sc, front lp sc in each sc across, ch 1, turn. (65 [67, 69, 71, 73, 73, 73] sc)

Rows 6–9 [6–9, 6–11, 6–11, 6–13, 6–13, 6–13]: [Rep rows 4 and 5 alternately] 2 [2, 3, 3, 4, 4, 4] times. (59 [61, 60, 62, 61, 61, 61] sc at end of last row)

Row 10 [10, 12, 12, 14, 14, 14]: Rep row 4. (58 [60, 59, 61, 60, 60, 60] sc)

Rows 11–15 [11–19, 13–21, 13–25, 15–29, 15–33, 15–37]: Ch 1, front lp sc in each sc across, turn.

Row 16 [20, 22, 26, 30, 34, 38]: Ch 1, front lp sc in each sc across, 2 front lp sc in last sc, turn. (59 [61, 60, 62, 61, 61, 61] sc)

Row 17 [21, 23, 27, 31, 35, 39]: Ch 3, sc in 2nd ch from hook, sc in next ch, front lp sc in each sc across, ch 1, turn. (61 [63, 62, 64, 63, 63, 63] sc)

Rows 18–23 [22–27, 24–31, 28–35, 32–41, 36–45, 40–49]: [Rep last 2 rows alternately] 3 [3, 4, 4, 5, 5, 5] times. (70 [72, 74, 76, 78, 78, 78] sc at end of last row)

Row 24 [28, 32, 36, 42, 46, 50]: Ch 1, front lp sc in each sc across to last sc, 2 front lp sc in last sc, ch 38 [44, 48, 54, 60, 68, 76], working in unused lps of foundation ch, 2 sc in next ch, sc in each ch across, turn.

Right Shoulder

Row 1: Ch 1, *front lp sc in each sc across** to ch, sc in each ch, rep from * to **, turn. (180 [190, 198, 208, 218, 226, 234] sc)

Rows 2–5: Ch 1, front lp sc in each sc across, turn.

Row 6: Ch 1, working in front lps only of sts, *sc in next sc, dc in next sc, rep from * 43 [46, 48, 50, 53, 55, 57] times, (front lp sc, dc) in each of next 2 sc, **sc in next sc, dc in next sc, rep from ** across to last sc, hdc in last sc, turn. (182 [192, 200, 210, 220, 228, 236] sts)

Rows 7–14 [7–14, 7–14, 7–14, 7–16, 7–16, 7–16]: Ch 1, work in **lace pattern** (see Pattern Stitch) across, turn.

Row 15 [15, 15, 15, 17, 17, 17]: Ch 1, work in lace pattern in first 80 [84, 88, 93, 97, 101, 105] sts, front lp sc in each of next 17 [19, 19, 19, 21, 21, 21] sts, work in lace pattern across, turn.

Row 16 [16, 16, 16, 18, 18, 18]: Ch 1, work in lace pattern in first 82 [86, 90, 95, 99, 103, 107] sts, front lp sc in each of next 23 [25, 25, 25, 27, 27, 27] sts, work in lace pattern across, turn.

Row 17 [17, 17, 17, 19, 19, 19]: Ch 1, work in lace pattern in first 76 [80, 84, 89, 93, 97, 101] sts, front lp sc in each of next 24 [26, 26, 26, 28, 28, 28] sts, work in lace pattern across, turn.

Row 18 [18, 18, 18, 20, 20, 20]: Ch 1, work in lace pattern in first 82 [86, 90, 95, 99, 103, 107] sts, front lp sc in each of next 27 [29, 29, 31, 31, 31] sts, work in lace pattern across, turn.

Row 19 [19, 19, 19, 21, 21, 21]: Ch 1, work in lace pattern in first 73 [77, 81, 86, 90, 94, 98] sts, front lp sc in each of next 27 [29, 29, 29,

 American School of Needlework • Berne, Indiana 46711 • DRGnetwork.com

31, 31, 31] sts, work in lace pattern across, turn.

Back

Row 1: Ch 1, work in lace pattern in first 81 [85, 89, 94, 98, 102, 106] sts, front lp sc in each of next 6 sts, turn. *(87 [91, 95, 100, 104, 108, 112] sts)*

Row 2: Ch 1, sc dec in first 2 sc, front lp sc in each of next 5 sts, work in lace pattern across, turn. *(86 [90, 94, 99, 103, 107, 113] sts)*

Row 3: Ch 1, work in lace pattern in first 80 [84, 88, 93, 97, 101, 105] sts, front lp sc in each of next 4 sc, sc dec in last 2 sc, turn. *(85 [89, 93, 98, 102, 106, 112] sts)*

Row 4: Ch 1, front lp sc in each of first 5 sc, work in lace pattern across, turn.

Row 5: Ch 1, work in lace pattern in first 80 [84, 88, 93, 97, 101, 105] sts, front lp sc in each of last 5 sc, turn.

Rows 6–15 [6–19, 6–23, 6–27, 6–27, 6–31, 6–35]: [Rep rows 4 and 5 alternately] 5 [7, 9, 11, 11, 13, 15] times.

Row 16 [20, 24, 28, 28, 32, 36]: Rep row 4.

Row 17 [21, 25, 29, 33, 37]: Ch 1, work in lace pattern in first 81 [85, 89, 94, 98, 102, 106] sts, front lp sc in each of next 3 sc, 2 front lp sc in last sc, fasten off.

Front

Row 1: Join yarn with sl st in last front lp sc of row 1 of Back, front lp sc in each of next 24 [26, 26, 26, 28, 28, 28] sts on front side of Right Shoulder, work in lace pattern across, turn.

Row 2: Ch 1, work in lace pattern in first 70 [74, 78, 83, 87, 91, 95] sts, front lp sc in each of next 5 sc, sc dec in last 2 sc, turn.

Row 3: Ch 1, front lp sc in each of first 5 sc, work in lace pattern across, turn.

Row 4: Ch 1, work in lace pattern in first 70 [74, 78, 83, 87, 91, 95] sts, front lp sc in each of next 5 sc, turn.

Rows 5–16 [5–20, 5–24, 5–28, 5–28, 5–32, 5–36]: [Rep rows 3 and 4 alternately] 6 [8, 10, 12, 12, 14, 16] times.

Row 17 [21, 25, 29, 29, 33, 37]: Rep row 3.

Row 18 [22, 26, 30, 30, 34, 38]: Ch 1, work in lace pattern in first 71 [75, 79, 84, 88, 92, 96] sts, front lp sc in each of next 4 sc, 2 front lp sc in next sc, ch 18 [20, 20, 20, 22, 22, 22], 2 front lp sc in first sc of Back, front lp sc in each of next 4 sc, work in lace pattern across, turn.

Left Shoulder

Row 1: Ch 1, work in lace pattern in first 81 [85, 89, 94, 98, 102, 106] sts, front lp sc in each of next 6 sts, sc in each of next 18 [20, 20, 20, 22, 22, 22] ch, front lp sc in each of next 6 sts, work in lace pattern across, turn.

Row 2: Ch 1, work in lace pattern in first 72 [76, 80, 85, 89, 93, 97] sts, front lp sc in each of next 30 sts, work in lace pattern across, turn.

Row 3: Ch 1, work in lace pattern in first 82 [86, 90, 95, 99, 103, 107] sts, front lp sc in each of next 26 sts, sc in next sc, work in lace pattern across, turn.

Row 4: Ch 1, work in lace pattern in first 77 [81, 85, 90, 94, 98, 102] sts, front lp sc in each of next 25 sts, work in lace pattern across, turn.

Row 5: Ch 1, work in lace pattern in first 82 [86, 90, 95, 99, 103, 107] sts, front lp sc in each of next 25 sts, work in lace pattern across, turn.

Row 6: Ch 1, work in lace pattern in first 80 [84, 88, 93, 97, 101, 105] sts, front lp sc in each of next 19 sts, work in lace pattern across, turn.

Rows 7–13 [7–13, 7–13, 7–13, 7–15, 7–15, 7–15]: Ch 1, work in lace pattern across, turn.

Row 14 [14, 14, 14, 16, 16, 16]: Ch 1, work in lace pattern in first 88 [94, 98, 102, 108, 112, 116] sts, [sc dec in next 2 sts] twice, work in lace pattern across, turn.

Rows 15–19 [15–19, 15–19, 15–19, 17–21, 17–21, 17–21]: Ch 1, front lp sc in each st across, turn.

Left Side Panel

Row 1: Ch 1, front lp sc in each of first 70 [72, 74, 76, 78, 78, 78] sts, turn. *(70 [72, 74, 76, 78, 78, 78] sc)*

Row 2: Ch 1, sc dec in first 2 sc, front lp sc in each sc across, turn. *(69 [71, 73, 75, 77, 77, 77] sc)*

Row 3: Ch 1, front lp sc in each sc across to last 2 sc, sc dec in last 2 sc, turn. *(68 [70, 72, 74, 76, 76, 76] sc)*

Row 4: Ch 1, sc dec in first 2 sc, sc dec in next 2 sc, front lp sc in each sc across, turn. *(66 [68, 70, 72, 74, 74, 74] sc)*

Row 5: Ch 1, front lp sc in each sc across to last 2 sc, sc dec in last 2 sc, turn. *(65 [67, 69, 71, 73, 73, 73] sc)*

Rows 6–9 [6–9, 6–11, 6–11, 6–13, 6–13, 6–13]: [Rep rows 4 and 5 alternately] 2 [2, 3, 3, 4, 4, 4] times. *(59 [61, 60, 62, 61, 61, 61] sc at end of last row)*

Row 10 [10, 12, 12, 14, 14, 14]: Rep row 2. *(58 [60, 59, 61, 60, 60, 60] sc)*

Rows 11–15 [11–19, 13–21, 13–25, 15–29, 15–33, 15–37]: Ch 1, front lp sc in each sc across, turn.

Row 16 [20, 22, 26, 30, 34, 38]: Ch 3, sc in 2nd ch from hook, sc in next ch, front lp sc in each sc across, turn. *(60 [62, 61, 63, 62, 62, 62] sc)*

Row 17 [21, 23, 27, 31, 35, 39]: Ch 1, front lp sc in each sc across to last sc, 2 front lp sc in last sc, turn. *(61 [63, 62, 64, 63, 63, 63] sc)*

Rows 18–23 [22–27, 24–31, 28–35, 32–41, 36–45, 40–49]: [Rep last 2 rows alternately] 3 [3, 4, 4, 5, 5, 5] times. *(70 [72, 74, 76, 78, 78, 78] sc at end of last row)*

Row 24 [28, 32, 36, 42, 46, 50]: Hold piece with WS of Left Side Panel and RS of Left Shoulder facing, working in

front lps of both pieces at same time, sc in front lp of first sc on Left Side Panel and front lp of corresponding sc of Left Shoulder, front lp sc in each st across, **do not fasten off**.

Edgings
Lower Edging
Ch 1, working in ends of rows around outer edge, sc in each row around, sl st in first sc, fasten off.

Front Neckline Edging
Hold piece with WS of front neckline facing, join yarn with sl st in last st of Right Shoulder, working in ends of rows, sc in each row across, sl st in first st of Left Shoulder, fasten off.

Back Neckline Edging
Hold piece with WS of back neck edge facing, join yarn with sl st in last st of Left Shoulder, working in ends of rows, sc in each row across, sl st in first st of Right Shoulder, fasten off.

Armhole Edging
Hold 1 Sleeve with WS facing, join yarn with sl st in last st of Shoulder, working in ends of rows, sc in each row across, join in first st of Shoulder, fasten off. Rep on other armhole. ■

General Information

Standard Yarn Weight System
Categories of yarn, gauge ranges, and recommended hook sizes

Yarn Weight Symbol & Category Names	1 SUPER FINE	2 FINE	3 LIGHT	4 MEDIUM	5 BULKY	6 SUPER BULKY
Type of Yarns in Category	Sock, Fingering, Baby	Sport, Baby	DK, Light Worsted	Worsted, Afghan, Aran	Chunky, Craft, Eyelash, Rug	Super Chunky, Roving
Crochet Gauge* Ranges in Single Crochet to 4 inch	21–32 sts	16–20 sts	12–17 sts	11–14 sts	8–11 sts	5–9 sts
Recommended Hook in Metric Size Range	2.25–3.25mm	3.5–4.5mm	4.5–5.5mm	5.5–6.5mm	6.5–9mm	9mm and larger
Recommended Hook U.S. Size Range	B/1–E/4	E/4–7	7–I/9	I/9–K/10½	K/10½–M/13	M/13 and larger

* GUIDELINES ONLY: The above reflect the most commonly used gauges and hook sizes for specific yarn categories.

Stitch Guide

For more complete information, visit **FreePatterns.com**

Abbreviations

beg	begin/beginning
bpdc	back post double crochet
bpsc	back post single crochet
bptr	back post treble crochet
CC	contrasting color
ch	chain stitch
ch-	refers to chain or space previously made (i.e., ch-1 space)
ch sp	chain space
cl	cluster
cm	centimeter(s)
dc	double crochet
dec	decrease/decreases/decreasing
dtr	double treble crochet
fpdc	front post double crochet
fpsc	front post single crochet
fptr	front post treble crochet
g	gram(s)
hdc	half double crochet
inc	increase/increases/increasing
lp(s)	loop(s)
MC	main color
mm	millimeter(s)
oz	ounce(s)
pc	popcorn
rem	remain/remaining
rep	repeat(s)
rnd(s)	round(s)
RS	right side
sc	single crochet
sk	skip(ped)
sl st	slip stitch
sp(s)	space(s)
st(s)	stitch(es)
tog	together
tr	treble crochet
trtr	triple treble crochet
WS	wrong side
yd(s)	yard(s)
yo	yarn over

Chain—ch: Yo, pull through lp on hook.

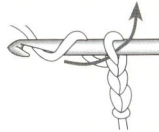

Slip stitch—sl st: Insert hook in st, pull through both lps on hook.

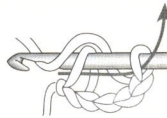

Single crochet—sc: Insert hook in st, yo, pull through st, yo, pull through both lps on hook.

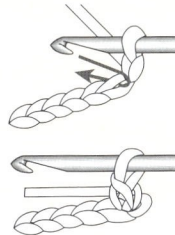

Front post stitch—fp: Back post stitch—bp: When working post st, insert hook from right to left around post st on previous row.

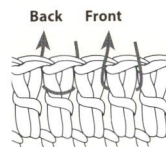

Back   Front

Front loop—front lp Back loop— back lp

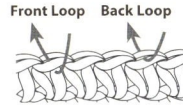

Front Loop   Back Loop

Half double crochet—hdc: Yo, insert hook in st, yo, pull through st, yo, pull through all 3 lps on hook.

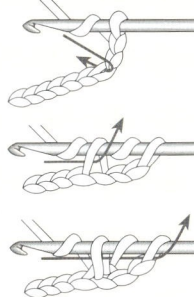

Double crochet—dc: Yo, insert hook in st, yo, pull through st, [yo, pull through 2 lps] twice.

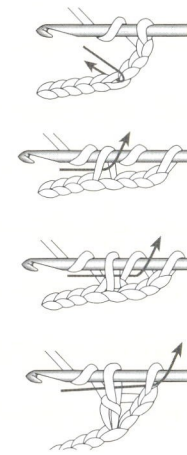

Change colors: Drop first color; with 2nd color, pull through last 2 lps of st.

Treble crochet—tr: Yo twice, insert hook in st, yo, pull through st, [yo, pull through 2 lps] 3 times.

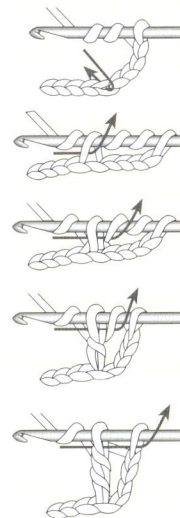

Double treble crochet—dtr: Yo 3 times, insert hook in st, yo, pull through st, [yo, pull through 2 lps], 4 times.

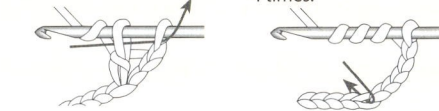

Single crochet decrease (sc dec): (Insert hook, yo, draw lp through) in each of the sts indicated, yo, draw through all lps on hook.

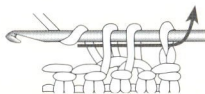

Example of 2-sc dec

Half double crochet decrease (hdc dec): (Yo, insert hook, yo, draw lp through) in each of the sts indicated, yo, draw through all lps on hook.

Example of 2-hdc dec

Double crochet decrease (dc dec): (Yo, insert hook, yo, draw loop through, draw through 2 lps on hook) in each of the sts indicated, yo, draw through all lps on hook.

Example of 2-dc dec

Treble crochet decrease (tr dec): Holding back last lp of each st, tr in each of the sts indicated, yo, pull through all lps on hook.

US		UK
sl st (slip stitch)	=	sc (single crochet)
sc (single crochet)	=	dc (double crochet)
hdc (half double crochet)	=	htr (half treble crochet)
dc (double crochet)	=	tr (treble crochet)
tr (treble crochet)	=	dtr (double treble crochet)
dtr (double treble crochet)	=	ttr (triple treble crochet)
skip	=	miss

How to Check Gauge

A correct stitch-gauge is very important. Please take the time to work a stitch-gauge swatch about 4 x 4 inches. Measure the swatch. If the number of stitches and rows is fewer than indicated under "Gauge" in the pattern, your hook is too large. Try another swatch with a smaller size hook. If the number of stitches and rows is more than indicated under "Gauge" in the pattern, your hook is too small. Try another swatch with a larger size hook.

Symbols

* An asterisk (or double asterisk **) is used to mark the beginning of a portion of instructions to be repeated; thus, "rep from * twice" means, after working the instructions once, repeat the instructions following the asterisk twice more (3 times in all).

[] Brackets are used to enclose instructions that should be worked the exact number of times specified immediately following the brackets, such as "[2 sc in next dc, sc in next dc] twice."

( ) Parentheses are used to set off a group of stitches to be worked all in one stitch, space or loop.

{ } Braces are used to set off the text to be repeated within the brackets or parentheses.

Skill Levels

BEGINNER
Beginner projects for first-time crocheters using basic stitches. Minimal shaping.

EASY
Easy projects using basic stitches, repetitive stitch patterns, simple color changes and simple shaping and finishing.

INTERMEDIATE
Intermediate projects with a variety of stitches, mid-level shaping and finishing.

EXPERIENCED
Experienced projects using advanced techniques and stitches, detailed shaping and refined finishing.

American School of Needlework®
excellence in instruction

TOLL-FREE ORDER LINE or to request a free catalog (800) 582-6643
Customer Service (800) 282-6643, **Fax** (800) 882-6643

Visit DRGnetwork.com.

We have made every effort to ensure the accuracy and completeness of these instructions.
We cannot, however, be responsible for human error, typographical mistakes or variations in individual work.

ISBN: 978-1-59012-219-8   All rights reserved.   Printed in USA   1 2 3 4 5 6 7 8 9